The Time . . . The Place

Readings for Lent and Advent

First published in 2009 by
Shield Books
© The Salvation Army
UK Territory Literary Unit
101 Newington Causeway
London SE1 6BN

ISBN 978-0-85412-797-9

This book of readings for Lent and Advent takes its inspiration from various sources: the Bible, the songbook and Salvation Army poets and writers. Lieut-Colonel Peter Dalziel has illustrated the poems which are used for the Saturday readings and he also created the picture for the front cover. He says: 'I have taken the hour glass as representation of passing time and the fact that the character is literally standing in "the sand of time" indicates that the time and place we find ourselves is "Now". God wants us to live our lives here and now by his grace and in his strength. The character is therefore holding his/her hands to the light. However, the question is are the hands raised in petition or in adoration and praise? Maybe all three.

All Bible readings from the *New International Version* unless otherwise stated

Abbreviations used

    KS – *Keep Singing*
    SASB – *The Song Book of The Salvation Army* (1986 edition)
    GNB – *Good News Bible*
    KJV – *King James Version*
    NEB – *New English Bible*
    NIV – *New International Version*

SHIELD
BOOKS
© The Salvation Army
United Kingdom Territory with
the Republic of Ireland

Contents

Lent

Advent

Week One

Week Two

Week Three

Lent

Week One

Ash Wednesday – Choosing to let God work in you

Bible reading: Psalm 51

'Create in me a pure heart, O God, and renew a steadfast spirit within me' (Psalm 51:10).

As we enter this time of preparation for Easter, let us ask God to create in us a pure heart and a steadfast spirit. We can take time to look at our lives with God and say to him: 'See for yourself whether I've done anything wrong – then guide me on the road to eternal life' (Psalm 139:24 The Message).

With my faint, weary soul to be made fully whole,
And thy perfect salvation to see,
With my heart all aglow to be washed white as snow,
I am coming, dear Saviour, to thee.

*I'm coming, I'm coming, dear Saviour, to thee,
With my heart all aglow to be washed white as snow,
I'm coming, dear Saviour, to thee.*

I thy promise believe, that in thee I shall live,
Through thy blood shed so freely for me;
To obtain a pure heart and secure the good part,
I am coming, dear Saviour, to thee.

All to thee now I give, thine to die, thine to live,
Crucified to the world e'er to be;
To be dead unto sin, with a new life within,
I am coming, dear Saviour, to thee.

To be thine, wholly thine, precious Saviour divine,
With my all consecrated to thee,
To be kept every hour by thy love's wondrous power,
I am coming, dear Saviour, to thee.

(SASB 469)

Personal Reflection

Dear Lord

I pray that you will cleanse me and make me a fit place to be your dwelling. Make my heart pure and keep me from all that might harm me or turn me away from you. Thank you, Lord, that I am born again and that I am a child of God. Keep me faithful in all I say and do. Amen.

Thursday – Choosing to allow God to lead you in his paths

Bible readings: Psalm 25:4-6; Jeremiah 6:16; Matthew 7:13-14

'Stand at the crossroads and look; ask for the ancient paths, ask where the good way is, and walk in it, and you will find rest for your souls' (Jeremiah 6:16).

We are on a spiritual journey, both during this time of Lent and throughout our Christian lives. We can ask God for guidance and help so that we will keep on the right path. Some of us may be at a crossroads right now. Let us remember to ask where the good way is and then have the courage to walk in it.

As the varied way of life we journey,
Come the plains and then the mountainside,
Come the days of joy when birds are singing,
And the world is fair and sweet and wide;
Then a deeper joy comes, overfilling,
From the everlasting throne of love,
And all other joy is but an echo
From the ever-blessèd heights above.

There are shadows on the earthly pathway
Where, at times uncertainly, we tread;
In perplexity we halt and linger
Till our faith again is upward led.
For the heights of truth are ever calling,
And celestial radiance from afar
On our pilgrim way is gently falling
For our comfort where the shadows are.

In the days of peace and golden sunshine,
In the days of joy, or days of woe,
There is confidence in him who holds us;
There is light to guide us here below.
And beyond await the heights of rapture
Where all earthly joys, transcended, fade
In the glory of the Saviour's presence,
In the home eternal he has made.

(*SASB* 711)

Personal Reflection

Dear Lord

I do not know what my future holds but I know that I can trust you completely. I thank you that you and I are on this journey together. Be my guide, Lord, and lead me to the future you have planned for me. Amen.

Friday – Choosing to live in the light

Bible readings: Psalm 43:3-5; John 1:1-5; John 3:16-21; John 8:12

'Send forth your light and your truth, let them guide me' (Psalm 43:3).

Sometimes it is tempting to despair when we look at how dark the world is that we live in. But if we keep our eyes fixed on Jesus we can live and walk in his light. And, more than that, we can be a light for other people. Jesus told us to let our light shine before men – we pray that people will see Jesus' light in our lives.

> Walk in the light: so shalt thou know
> That fellowship of love
> His Spirit only can bestow,
> Who reigns in light above.
>
> Walk in the light: and thou shalt find
> Thy heart made truly his
> Who dwells in cloudless light enshrined,
> In whom no darkness is.
>
> Walk in the light: and thou shalt own
> Thy darkness passed away,
> Because that light hath on thee shone
> In which is perfect day.
>
> Walk in the light: and e'en the tomb
> No fearful shade shall wear;
> Glory shall chase away its gloom,
> For Christ hath conquered there.

Walk in the light: and thine shall be
A path, though thorny, bright;
For God, by grace, shall dwell in thee,
And God himself is light.

(SASB 465)

Personal Reflection

Dear Lord

Help me to walk in your light and to be a guiding light to others who are still walking in darkness. Amen.

Saturday – 'Perspective' by Clifford W. Kew

Not often do I raise my eyes and look afar.
I lose so much – for that is where life's blessings are.
There is no scenery without the far horizon.
Distant drab details make a view to feast the eyes on;
The random trees become a wood;
Untidy grass is there a field;

An ugly wall becomes a feature of the view.
Too often is my gaze around my feet.
I see the clogging mud, the sun-dried dust,
Scar of new building, or old metal's rust.
If this were all there was to see,
'Twould matter little had we blinded eyes.
Yet, from afar, 'tis all a paradise.

When astronauts survey the shrinking world,
And see its beauty from afar,
No scar of earthquake, flood, or blight of war
Assaults the eyes.
They see the beauty of creation,
Not local devastation.

Lord, let me look at life with longer sight;
Let not my view be hardships of this day,
Cares of the present, burdens that will pass.
Focus my eyes, that, far beyond the moment,
I may see 'now' as part of *all* you'll make of me,
Part of the eternal me,
Of your whole plan for me.

Something To Do

Thinking about the theme of making choices, write a poem about how you have had to make choices in your life.

Perspective

'There is no scenery without the far horizon'

1st Sunday – Good, Better, Best

Autograph albums were one of the passing crazes when I was young. All of us would pester everyone we knew to scribble a line or two in our albums.

It was the quantity of contributions we collected that counted, rather than the quality. After all, 'By hook or by crook I'll be last in this book' doesn't exactly rate as immortal poetry, does it?

But among all the 'verse and worse' in my album were four lines – I forget whose contribution they were – which, without any effort on my part, remained fixed in my memory:

> Good, better, best,
> Never let it rest,
> Till your good is better
> And your better best.

As a literary effort it wouldn't make *The Oxford Book Of English Verse*, but it does add a vital dimension to the choices Christians have to make.

Christians of long standing can be so accustomed to thinking only of the black-and-white choice between good and evil that they don't see the more subtle choices between good, better and best.

This subtle choice was the kind that Jesus had to make at the beginning of his ministry. His baptism, in which he both identified with sinful man (for John's was the baptism of repentance) and also received confirmation of his divine nature, was the crossroads of his life (see Mark 1:4, 9-11).

It is hardly surprising that Jesus withdrew at the Holy Spirit's prompting (Luke 4:1) to consider the implications of his ministry and to fix its priorities. All kinds of questions must have been hammering in his mind.

How would his ministry fit into the popular belief that the coming Messiah would be a powerful political figure who would restore Israel's national status? Was it right to use any means to justify the end of establishing God's Kingdom on earth? What was the right balance between ministering to the suffering of the body and forgiving the sins of the soul?

The Devil knew his quarry too well to make the mistake of offering Jesus easy good-or-evil alternatives. Using Scripture to back his subtle tactics (for, strangely, good can be used as a weapon to achieve evil ends), he tried to persuade Jesus to stop at what was merely good, rather than opt for the best.

The first choice presented to Jesus was between meeting men's physical hunger and offering them the bread of life (see Luke 4:3-4; John 6:35).

Of course Jesus wanted to feed the hungry and relieve their suffering! We who have been profoundly moved by television pictures of starving children can understand that. But, in recognising that 'man cannot live by bread alone', Jesus chose the best and not simply the good.

That is not to say that, from then on, he refused to feed the hungry and offer a ministry of compassion and social concern. But, in becoming aware of the difference between the good and the best, Jesus strengthened his ministry and was able to merge a social and spiritual concern – with no artificial division between the two.

The second choice offered to Jesus involved making a compromise. 'You want power over people?' the Devil suggested in effect. 'Then just lower your standards a little and you can have it.'

But Jesus realised that power without principle is dangerous. It's a fact that history has proved over and over again. Only power that acknowledges the supreme authority of God can achieve any good end.

Jesus' answer made it clear that he rejected compromise and chose the best: 'The Scripture says, "Worship the Lord your God and serve only him!"'

The final decision concerned how Jesus was going to use his God-given status and power. One spectacular miracle and people would be eating out of his hand. He could bring about God's Heaven on earth with just one leap of faith (see Luke 4:9-12).

But Jesus was not deceived. His insight into human nature, much of it gained from the 30 hidden years before beginning his ministry, told him that spectacular methods are not necessarily the best. Easy come, easy go might have been the result of a ministry based solely on miraculous powers.

Much of his ministry was to be among individuals. He ministered by challenging a fisherman, befriending a tax-collector, compassionately touching a leper, counselling an outcast woman and talking intimately with a disciple shamed by failure.

His decisions made, Jesus began his ministry confident that he was doing God's will in God's way. But, significantly, Luke's Gospel comments, 'When the devil finished tempting Jesus in every way, he left him *for a while*.'

Jesus would constantly need to check that his priorities remained the same as they were in this testing time, that his ministry ran parallel to the will of God.

The choices facing Jesus still face the Church and individual Christians. They are choices between the good, the better and the best.

Jean Bryant

Week Two

Monday – Challenged to discover the truth

Bible readings: Psalm 86:1-12; John 14:1-7; John 8:31-32

'Teach me your way, O Lord, and I will walk in your truth; give me an undivided heart, that I may fear your name' (Psalm 86:11).

The truth Jesus brought the world is not relative. There aren't any grey areas, where his truth is open to personal interpretation. Jesus told the world that he was the truth which would lead people to God. Pilate may have asked, 'What is truth?' Jesus said, 'I am the way and the truth and the life.' The truth is: 'God so loved the world that he gave his one and only Son, that whoever believes in him shall not perish but have eternal life' (John 3:16).

> Beyond the farthest bounds of earth,
> Beyond the ocean's line,
> Beyond the starlit universe
> We sense a power divine.
>
> The lines and circles, planes and arcs
> Which we by science trace
> All indicate a master mind,
> Its beauty, truth and grace.
>
> Like searching eyes earth's telescopes
> The fiery heavens scan;
> And now the music of the spheres
> Is heard by listening man.

Lord, as we seek for vaster truth,
And as our spaceships soar,
Help us to recognise your might
And praise your mercy more.

For you, who set the ordinance
Of worlds beyond our sight,
Have given us minds desiring truth
And hearts that know delight.

Lord, teach us in your only Son
To reach the way we dream,
To follow truth as he knew truth,
And find the life supreme.

(*SASB* 27)

Personal Reflection

Dear Lord

Thank you that we can follow you in confidence, assured that you are the way, and the truth and the life. Help us to live lives that show to others just what believing in you means. Amen.

Tuesday – Challenged to believe

Bible readings: John 1:10-13; John 3:16-21; John 5:24; John 11:25-26

'I tell you the truth, whoever hears my word and believes him who sent me has eternal life and will not be condemned; he has crossed over from death to life' (John 5:24).

To believe in Jesus Christ as Lord and Saviour means having the promise of eternal life. Sometimes it isn't easy to hold on to faith and belief in a dark and faithless world. But we don't believe in Jesus because we need a crutch to lean on; we believe in Jesus because he makes sense of everything that we are and everything that we do. We may find it hard to believe because we have never seen our Lord in the flesh but Jesus said: 'Blessed are those who have not seen and yet have believed' (John 20:29).

> Out of my darkness God called me,
> Out of the depth of my night,
> Out of the shadows of sorrow,
> Into the life of his light.
>
> Out of my darkness he called me,
> Out of my doubt, my despair,
> Out of the wastes of my winter,
> Into the spring of his care.
>
> Out of my darkness he called me
> Into his sunshining day,
> Out of my gloom to his glory;
> What could I do but obey?

Out of your darkness he calls you,
Out of your doubt, your despair,
Out of the wastes of your winter,
Into the spring of his care.

(SASB 378)

Personal Reflection

Dear Lord

Thank you for calling us out of the darkness into your light. Help us not to live as if we were still lost in the dark. Thank you, too, for making sense of everything that we are and do and for caring for us so deeply. Amen.

Wednesday – Challenged to follow Jesus

Bible Readings: Matthew 4:18-20; Matthew 16:24-25; John 8:12; Romans 15:5-6

'When Jesus spoke again to the people, he said, "I am the light of the world. Whoever follows me will never walk in darkness, but will have the light of life"' (John 8:12).

Following Jesus may not be easy – but when we do follow him it means that we are following God's plan for our lives. It also means we are walking in the light shed by our Lord. And even when we go through difficult times we still have the assurance that Jesus will never be absent from our lives.

Down in the valley with my Saviour I would go,
Where the flowers are blooming and the sweet waters flow;
Everywhere he leads me I would follow, follow on,
Walking in his footsteps till the crown be won.

Follow, follow, I will follow Jesus,
Anywhere, everywhere, I will follow on;
Follow, follow, I will follow Jesus,
Everywhere he leads me I will follow on.

Down in the valley with my Saviour I would go,
Where the storms are sweeping and the dark waters flow;
With his hand to lead me I will never, never fear;
Dangers cannot fright me if my Lord is near.

Down in the valley, or upon the mountain steep,
Close beside my Saviour would my soul ever keep;
He will lead me safely in the path that he has trod,
Up to where they gather on the hills of God.

(SASB 483)

Personal Reflection

Dear Lord

We know that sometimes we will have to go through difficult times. It is part of being human. Help us to trust you, especially when the going gets really rough. Amen.

Thursday – Challenged to worship

Bible readings: 1 Chronicles 16:23-36; Psalm 100; John 4:23-24

'Shout for joy to the Lord, all the earth. Worship the Lord with gladness; come before him with joyful songs' (Psalm 100:1-2).

When we worship God we should delight in being in his presence. He wants us to spend quality time with him and takes delight in us too. We can worship in lots of different ways but when we leave a time of worship we should take with us the knowledge that we have been close to God and he has been close to us.

> O worship the Lord in the beauty of holiness!
> Bow down before him, his glory proclaim;
> With gold of obedience, and incense of lowliness,
> Kneel and adore him, the Lord is his name.
>
> Low at his feet lay thy burden of carefulness,
> High on his heart he will bear it for thee,
> Comfort thy sorrows and answer thy prayerfulness,
> Guiding thy steps as may best for thee be.
>
> Fear not to enter his courts in the slenderness
> Of the poor wealth thou would'st reckon as thine;
> Truth in its beauty, and love in its tenderness,
> These are the offerings to lay on his shrine.

These, though we bring them in trembling and fearfulness,
He will accept for the name that is dear;
Mornings of joy give for evenings of tearfulness,
Trust for our trembling, and hope for our fear.

O worship the Lord in the beauty of holiness!
Bow down before him, his glory proclaim;
With gold of obedience, and incense of lowliness,
Kneel and adore him, the Lord is his name.

(*SASB* 183)

Personal Reflection

Dear Lord

Teach us to worship you in beauty and in truth and may
every time of worship draw us closer to you. Thank you for
the privilege of being able to enter your presence. Help us
not to take this for granted. Amen.

Friday – Challenged to witness

Bible readings: Psalm 19:1-4; 1 Peter 2:9-10;
Luke 24:46-48; Mark 16:15; Acts 5:42

'The heavens declare the glory of God; the skies proclaim
the work of his hands. Day after day they pour forth
speech; night after night they display knowledge. There is
no speech or language where their voice is not heard. Their
voice goes out into all the earth, their words to the ends of
the world' (Psalm 19:1-4).

*All of God's creation witnesses to the power of the Creator.
As people of God, saved by grace and through the sacrifice
of Jesus, we have to witness as well. When we know the
truth for ourselves we have to tell others. We don't
necessarily have to use words – we can witness by
everything that we are and do.*

> Joyful, joyful, we adore thee,
> God of glory, Lord of love;
> Hearts unfold like flowers before thee,
> Hail thee as the sun above.
> Melt the clouds of sin and sadness,
> Drive the clouds of doubt away;
> Giver of immortal gladness,
> Fill us with the light of day.
>
> All thy works with joy surround thee,
> Earth and heaven reflect thy rays,
> Stars and angels sing around thee,
> Centre of unbroken praise;
> Field and forest, vale and mountain,

Blossoming meadow, flashing sea,
Chanting bird and flowing fountain
Call us to rejoice in thee.

Thou art giving and forgiving,
Ever blessing, ever blest,
Wellspring of the joy of living,
Ocean-depth of happy rest.
Thou the Father, Christ our brother –
All who live in love are thine;
Teach us how to love each other,
Lift us to the joy divine.

Mortals, join the mighty chorus
Which the morning stars began;
Father-love is reigning o'er us,
Brother-love binds man to man.
Ever singing, march we onward,
Victors in the midst of strife;
Joyful music lifts us sunward
In the triumph song of life.

(*SASB* 10)

Personal Reflection

Dear Lord

Help us not to be afraid to tell others about you. We shouldn't be afraid – or ashamed. You can do a glorious thing in the lives of everyone we speak to. Help us to remember that. Amen.

Saturday – 'For Their Sakes I Sanctify Myself'
by Mina Russell

If I could know
That self-abandonment in me
Would help a man who never yet had prayed,
To speak to God ————

If I could know
That giving self and time
Would bring the Christ to one who long had strayed
And lost his way ————

If I could know ahead of time,
I'd give myself!

Not time alone – he has my days;
Not skills – he taught me all I know that he can use;
Not strength – from him it comes each hour;

But, if I knew ahead of time
That it would count in bringing men to God,
I'd give my self, my will, my heart.
I'm sure I would.

But as I live from day to day
I do not know how much my offering counts
In helping those I see.
Sometimes I catch a glimpse of God
At work through me;
But I have learned a little of the way of love,
The path of faith,
The road Christ followed to the cross,
And I must follow him
For his, and for their sakes.

And as he died for those who would forsake,
And those who would deny,
As well as for the strong who followed to the death,
I, too, must set myself apart
For them, and for his sake,
Not knowing always what it means;
But sure that in this fellowship of love
I work with God!
And I can leave the end with him.

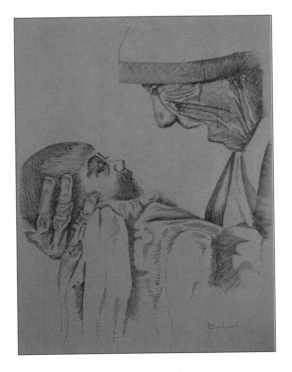

For their sakes

'Sometimes I catch a glimpse of God'

Something To Do

Write your own psalm of praise to God. Try illustrating the psalm with your own artwork or with a montage of pictures from other sources.

2nd Sunday – The Time … The Place

Choosing the right psychological moment to say something is a skill. When your wife has had a bad day with a crying baby, squabbling kids and a broken-down washing machine, don't expect the news that you are going on a three-day conference held in an exclusive country hotel will be met with an ecstatic kiss.

If your son has got bad grades in his exam and realises what a fool he was to waste revision time, it's not the right moment to say, 'I told you so' – if ever there is a right moment to do so, that is.

It's equally important to know how to say what needs to be said, as well as when to say it. It may be that 'the truth hurts', but even so there is no need for us to tell it in such a way as to leave a trail of corpses in our wake.

In both skills – choosing *when* and *how* to tell the truth – Jesus was an expert. 'I have much more to tell you,' he said to his disciples during his final meal with them, 'but now it would be too much for you to bear' (John 16:12, all references in this article from *Good News Bible*). He sensed that the moment was too tense to reveal the truth, even though he had very little time left for teaching.

So we can be sure that when Jesus revealed his identity, and the nature of his Messiahship, to his disciples, it was at the right time and in the right way.

The Jews believed that the Messiah would be a popular, national hero who would liberate the nation and restore it to its former power and glory, using force if necessary.

There's evidence that the disciples – who were men of their age – shared this belief. So, for example, they squabbled over who should have the place of importance in this coming kingdom (see Mark 9:33, 34; 10:35-45).

Jesus sensed that he was approaching a crisis. Although he was popular with the people, there was growing opposition from the Pharisees. And even his popularity had its dangers – 'You are looking for me because you ate the bread and had all you wanted, not because you understood my miracles,' he told the crowds who had wanted to make him king after he had fed them (John 6:26).

At the right time his disciples would have to know the truth about their hero – he was 'the suffering servant', rather than the popular image of the Messiah.

As they approached Caesarea Philippi, Jesus decided it was the right time to broach the subject. The growing opposition prompted it, and he needed time to repeat the truth again. He began by skilfully probing what they understood already.

'Who do people say that I am?' he asked, taking the temperature of popular belief. Progressing, he then asked, 'But what about you – who do *you* say I am?' (Mark 8:27, 29).

It was Peter who answered, showing that he had some realisation of who Jesus was.

But Jesus even then didn't bombard them with truth: 'Jesus *began* to teach his disciples: "The Son of Man must suffer much and be rejected. ... He will be put to death"' (Mark 8:31).

In spite of making it 'very clear' (verse 32), it was evident that Peter couldn't yet come to terms with the truth – it was so contrary to his beliefs.

Jesus realised that it was not going to be easy for the disciples to change, to accept this new, even unwelcome, idea. For that reason he continued to reveal the truth whenever the occasion arose (see Mark 9:30-32; 10:32-34; 10:45; 14:8; 22-31).

The truth, so painstakingly taught by Jesus, eventually found a place in Peter's own teaching: 'It was the costly sacrifice of Christ' (1 Peter 1:19); 'the living stone rejected by people' (2:4); 'for Christ himself suffered for you and left you an example. … Christ himself carried our sins in his body to the cross' (2:21, 24) are some of the phrases found in the First Epistle of Peter.

We can be sure that whenever Jesus reveals the truth, he will choose the right moment. And not only that, but also the right way. He will not bludgeon us with his revelation, but will make it shine into our minds, like a kindly light, as they slowly open to the truth.

Jean Bryant

Week Three

Monday – Committed to the planet

Bible Readings: Genesis 1:1-2; Genesis 1:26-31; Psalm 8

'In the beginning God created the heavens and the earth. Now the earth was formless and empty, darkness was over the surface of the deep, and the Spirit of God was hovering over the waters' (Genesis 1:1-2).

As the people of God, we have a responsibility to care for the whole of his creation. We need to be aware of the problems our planet is facing and do our best to take care of the world which God made for us to enjoy. Christians must not be guilty of complacency; we must stand up and be counted among those who care about the world.

All creatures of our God and King,
Lift up your voice and with us sing
Alleluia, alleluia!
Thou burning sun with golden beam,
Thou silver moon with softer gleam:

O praise him, O praise him,
Alleluia, alleluia, alleluia!

Thou rushing wind that art so strong,
Ye clouds that sail in heaven along,
O praise him, alleluia!
Thou rising morn, in praise rejoice,
Ye lights of evening, find a voice:
O praise him, Alleluia!

Thou flowing water, pure and clear,
Make music for thy Lord to hear,
Alleluia, alleluia!
Thou fire so masterful and bright,
That givest man both warmth and light:
O praise him, Alleluia!

Dear mother earth, who day by day
Unfoldest blessings on our way,
O praise him, alleluia!
The flowers and fruits that in thee grow,
Let them his glory also show:
O praise him, Alleluia!

Let all things their creator bless,
And worship him in humbleness,
O praise him, alleluia!
Praise, praise the Father, praise the Son,
And praise the Spirit, Three in One:
O praise him, Alleluia!

(SASB 2)

Personal Reflection

Dear Lord

Thank you for the incredible world we live in – for its
beauty and variety, its grandeur, its unexpectedness.
Forgive us for the times we have taken it for granted.
Awaken in us the desire to take care of our world. Amen.

Tuesday – Committed to people

Bible readings: Matthew 25:31-40; Luke 4:14-21; John 21:15-17

'The Spirit of the Lord is on me, because he has anointed me to preach good news to the poor. He has sent me to proclaim freedom for the prisoners and recovery of sight for the blind, to release the oppressed, to proclaim the year of the Lord's favour' (Luke 4:18-19).

Jesus was committed to people. He wanted people to be saved and to take their rightful place in the Kingdom as God's children. But he also left his followers a commission to take care of people – to feed the hungry, visit prisoners, look after the sick and so on. His mission statement recorded in Luke tells us what he was anointed to do. He now leaves those tasks to us.

What can I say to cheer a world of sorrow?
How bring back hope where men have sorely failed?
Just where I am I'll speak the word of comfort,
Tell how for me Christ's sacrifice availed.

Just where he needs me, my Lord has placed me,
Just where he needs me, there would I be!
And since he found me, by love he's bound me
To serve him joyfully.

What can I do to ease life's heavy burdens?
What can I do to help mankind in need?
Just where I am I'll share my neighbour's hardship,
Lighten his load, and prove a friend indeed.

What can I do to justify my living?
What can I be to make this life worthwhile?
I'll be a voice to call men to the Saviour,
Just where I am, and win my Father's smile.

(KS 93)

Personal Reflection

Dear Lord

There are so many people in the world who are hurting –
living in despair, with no hope of help or comfort. Help us to
remember that you have entrusted to us the task of
reaching out to others with your message of hope. You
have placed us just where you need us to do your work.
Thank you, Lord. Amen.

Wednesday – Committed to personal growth

Bible readings: Ephesians 4:7-16; Colossians 1:9-13;
2 Peter 1:3-8

'Make every effort to add to your faith goodness; and to
goodness knowledge; and to knowledge, self-control; and
to self-control, perseverance; and to perseverance,
godliness; and to godliness, brotherly kindness; and to
brotherly kindness, love. For if you possess these qualities
in increasing measure, they will keep you from being
ineffective and unproductive in your knowledge of our Lord
Jesus Christ' (2 Peter 1:5-8).

*As followers of Jesus, we are meant to grow in our faith.
There are many lessons to learn – but we have a Master
Teacher who is always there to help us with our lessons and
lead us on to the next stage. And there will never come a
time when we can say that we have learned all there is to
know. There are new pathways to explore, new avenues of
service to undertake every day.*

> Thou art the way, none other dare I follow;
> Thou art the truth, and thou hast made me free;
> Thou art the life, the hope of my tomorrow;
> Thou art the Christ who died for me.
> This is my creed, that 'mid earth's sin and sorrow,
> My life may guide men unto thee.

Hold thou my feet, let there be no returning
Along the path which thou hast bid me tread;
Train thou my mind, I would be ever learning
The better way thy fame to spread;
Keep thou my heart ablaze with holy burning
That love for souls may ne'er be dead.

I would bring peace to lives now torn asunder,
Ease aching hearts with words that soothe and heal;
I would bring peace when, breaking like the thunder,
Men rise in war, and hatred feel.
Peacemaker, Lord! Now I am stirred to wonder;
O take me, and my calling seal!

(SASB 529)

Personal Reflection

Dear Lord

Help us to be good students for there are so many lessons for us to learn. Thank you for being such a good and patient teacher. And, Lord, when we have learned what you have to teach us, help us to put our lessons to practical use. Amen.

Thursday – Committed to prayer

Bible readings: Matthew 6:9-13; Acts 2:42-43; Romans 12:12; Colossians 4:2; 1 Thessalonians 5:16-17; James 5:13-16

'Be joyful always; pray continually; give thanks in all circumstances, for this is God's will for you in Christ Jesus' (1 Thessalonians 5:16-17).

Prayer is a two-way communication with God. He wants us to talk to him and he also wants to talk to us. Prayer has remarkable power. It can change circumstances, it can change people, it can change us. As Christians, we should be committed to prayer. Let us pray.

> What a friend we have in Jesus,
> All our sins and griefs to bear!
> What a privilege to carry
> Everything to God in prayer!
> O what peace we often forfeit,
> O what needless pain we bear,
> All because we do not carry
> Everything to God in prayer!
>
> Have we trials and temptations?
> Is there trouble anywhere?
> We should never be discouraged:
> Take it to the Lord in prayer.
> Can we find a friend so faithful,
> Who will all our sorrows share?
> Jesus knows our every weakness:
> Take it to the Lord in prayer.

Are we weak and heavy laden,
Cumbered with a load of care?
Precious Saviour, still our refuge:
Take it to the Lord in prayer.
Do thy friends despise, forsake thee?
Take it to the Lord in prayer;
In his arms he'll take and shield thee,
Thou wilt find a solace there.

(SASB 645)

Personal Reflection

Dear Lord

What a power there is in prayer! And what a privilege it is to be able to pray, knowing that you always listen and understand. Answers may not always come in the way that we expect – but we know that you always answer. Amen.

Friday – Committed to peace

Bible readings: Isaiah 9:6-7; Isaiah 52:7; Matthew 5:9; John 14:27; John 16:33; Galatians 5:22-23; Colossians 3:12-15

'Peace I leave with you; my peace I give you. I do not give to you as the world gives. Do not let your hearts be troubled and do not be afraid' (John 14:27).

Jesus came to be a peace-bringer and he has entrusted to us the task of being peacemakers. It is not enough just to be passive. We have to make peace, bring it about. And peace should be more than just an absence of war; it should be a positive power for good, showing people that it is possible to live together in harmony, free from fear and hatred.

It came upon the midnight clear,
That glorious song of old,
From angels bending near the earth
To touch their harps of gold;
Peace on the earth, goodwill to men,
From Heaven's all-gracious King!
The world in solemn stillness lay
To hear the angels sing.

But with the woes of sin and strife
The world has suffered long;
Beneath the angel-strain have rolled
Two thousand years of wrong.
And man, at war with man, hears not
The love song which they bring;
O hush the noise, ye men of strife,
And hear the angels sing.

For lo! the days are hastening on,
By prophet bards foretold,
When with the ever-circling years
Comes round the age of gold,
When peace shall over all the earth
Its ancient splendours fling,
And the whole world give back the song
Which now the angels sing.

(*SASB* 83)

Personal Reflection

Dear Lord

Sometimes it seems as if the world will never be at peace again. We live in violent times and this unpeace seems to be affecting the whole of society. Please help us to be peacemakers wherever it is possible. Amen.

Saturday – 'Expressionless Death!' by Paul du Plessis

Love, to be love should be expressed,
If only by a gentle touch
Or merest shaping of a smile,
To prove the tender heart we claim.
Expressionless, our love will die.

Faith, to be faith should be expressed
In actions of the daily toil
Of serving, yet remaining meek
In lowly suffering with that faith.
Expressionless, our faith will die.

Forgiveness, too, should be expressed
In reconciling action which
Will bind once separated lives
In unity and fellowship.
Expressionless, forgiveness dies.

Hope, to be hope should be expressed
In looks of cheerful optimism
That even in despair sustain
The wearied soul near overcome.
Expressionless, our hope will die.

Thoughts will be thoughts and words are words.
Did these things alone suffice to tell
A doubting world that God was there?
Why then this Galilean Man
Expressing now that God is God?

Expressionless Death!

'If only by a gentle touch'

Something To Do

Draw around your hand several times and write the names of the people you pray for on the palms. Remember the Lord says: 'Can a mother forget the baby at her breast and have no compassion on the child she has borne? Though she may forget, I will not forget you! See, I have engraved you on the palms of my hands' (Isaiah 49:15-16).

3rd Sunday – There Is No Other Option

It's considered prudent to keep your options open these days. From business ventures through to marriage, we like to know where the escape button is located. We may not want to use it, but we just like to know it's there if necessary.

While it may be shrewd to keep our options open, it requires courage to commit ourselves to an action or relationship knowing that there's no going back, no escape button handy.

However, this doesn't mean that we need jump into situations foolhardily, particularly as Christians. Jesus recommended us to think things through, to weigh up situations before we act (see Luke 14:25-33). On another occasion he commented that the people of this world are sometimes much more shrewd in handling their affairs than the people of the light (Luke 16:8, all references in this article are from *Good News Bible*).

It seems that, although we ought to consider our options carefully before committing ourselves, once we have done it we shouldn't leave them open.

Roman Catholic priest Teilhard de Chardin was aware of this. As he committed himself to the priesthood he wrote: 'I am making a vow of poverty; never have I more clearly realised to what extent money can be a powerful means for the service and glorification of God. I am making a vow of chastity; never have I understood so well how a husband and wife complete each other in order better to advance to God. I am making a vow of obedience; never have I better understood what liberation there is in God's service. … But I have placed my trust in God, certain that he would grant me the grace to do his will in my life and to be faithful to my vows.'

In burning his boats behind him, Teilhard de Chardin was simply following Jesus' own example.

During his temptation Jesus had rejected any thought of compromise. Now the storm clouds were gathering. The Pharisees and Sadducees, normally at odds with each other, conveniently dropped their animosity and became united in their hostility towards Jesus. Even the ordinary people were now beginning to turn against him and his earlier popularity waned.

Jesus was aware of all this. He knew that if he were to take his ministry into Jerusalem, the centre of the Jewish world, it would mean certain death (see Luke 9:44, 51). But resolutely he set out towards Jerusalem and a head-on confrontation with his enemies. 'He went with no weapons but love, no resources but God and his own indomitable soul,' comments J. S. Stewart.

His disciples and other followers were afraid. Who wouldn't be in such a situation? Jesus warned them: 'We are going up to Jerusalem where the Son of Man will be handed over to the chief priests and teachers of the Law. They will condemn him to death and then hand him over to the Gentiles, who will mock him, spit on him, whip him and kill him' (Mark 10:33, 34).

Unlike Jesus, they wanted an escape button. And some of the followers used it. John's Gospel states that, after Jesus taught that his flesh and blood were the source of eternal life, many of his disciples complained that his teaching was too hard. 'Because of this, many of Jesus' followers turned back and would not go with him any more' (John 6:66).

A number of the early-day Salvation Army songs were written urging Salvationists to follow Jesus' example and follow determinedly after him, not allowing themselves even to think of faltering or giving up. Many pioneers needed tremendous courage, often being ostracised by family, friends and employers because of their resolve to follow Jesus through their Army service.

Some of the songs may even sound quaint today, but the temptation to keep our options open – albeit for different reasons – is just as strong. Perhaps we can't quite imagine ourselves singing, 'I'm a soldier if you want me, firm at my post I'll stay; Like all true Army heroes, I never run away.'

But we would agree with the truth, 'When you find the cross is heavy and you feel like giving in, take your weakness straight to Jesus, he will strengthen you within.'

For the Christian, it's the only option.

Jean Bryant

Week Four

Monday – Change of heart

Bible readings: 1 Samuel 16:7; Psalm 51:10-12; Psalm 139:23-24; Ezekiel 36:24-28; Matthew 5:8

'Create in me a pure heart, O God, and renew a steadfast spirit within me. Do not cast me from your presence or take your Holy Spirit from me. Restore to me the joy of your salvation and grant me a willing spirit, to sustain me' (Psalm 51:10-12).

Jesus said that we, as his followers, must love God with all our hearts, with all our souls and with all our minds. We must make sure that our hearts are right with him so we can fulfil this commandment. We need to allow God to examine our hearts and, if necessary, perform some spiritual surgery.

> O for a heart to praise my God,
> A heart from sin set free;
> A heart that always feels the blood
> So freely spilt for me.
>
> A heart resigned, submissive, meek,
> My great redeemer's throne;
> Where only Christ is heard to speak,
> Where Jesus reigns alone.
>
> A humble, lowly, contrite heart,
> Believing, true, and clean;
> Which neither life nor death can part
> From him that dwells within.

A heart in every thought renewed,
And full of love divine;
Perfect and right, and pure and good,
A copy, Lord, of thine.

Thy nature, gracious Lord, impart,
Come quickly from above;
Write thy new name upon my heart,
Thy new best name of love.

(SASB 444)

Personal Reflection

Dear Lord

As you look into my very being, I pray that you will see a believing, loving heart that is perfect, right and pure. If you see any sin in it, I ask that you will cleanse me from it. Write your name on my heart, Lord, so that I know that I really belong to you. Amen.

Tuesday – Change of priority

Bible readings: Joshua 24:14-15; Matthew 6:25-34

'Now fear the Lord and serve him with all faithfulness. Throw away the gods your forefathers worshipped beyond the River and in Egypt, and serve the Lord. But if serving the Lord seems undesirable to you, then choose for yourselves this day whom you will serve, whether the gods your forefathers served beyond the River, or the gods of the Amorites, in whose land you are living. But as for me and my household, we will serve the Lord' (Joshua 24:14-15).

Our priority as Christians should be seeking the will of God – and then doing it. When we have that right, then everything else should fall into place. Sometimes it is a question of making a conscious choice to follow God rather than our own ambitions or desires – but what he promises us makes that decision worthwhile.

O that in me the mind of Christ
A fixed abiding-place may find,
That I may know the will of God,
And live in him for lost mankind.

Doing the will of God,
Doing the will of God,
The best thing I know in this world below
Is doing the will of God.

The suffering servant he became,
Yea more; in loneliness and loss
He bore for me in grief and shame,
A crown of thorns, a heavy cross.

O that in me this mind might be,
The will of God be all my joy,
Prepared with him to go or stay,
My chief delight his sweet employ.

More than all else I would become
The servant of my servant-Lord;
My highest glory his reproach,
To do his will my best reward.

(SASB 451)

Personal Reflection

Dear Lord

Help me always to seek your will and then to do my best to carry it out. I want to be your faithful servant, Lord. I choose to follow you because that it is the best thing that anyone can do in this world. Amen.

Wednesday – Change of attitude

Bible readings: Ephesians 4:22-23; 2 Corinthians 5:17;
Philippians 2:1-11

'Therefore, if anyone is in Christ, he is a new creation; the
old has gone, the new has come!' (2 Corinthians 5:17).

*When we become Christians we find that our attitudes
towards all sorts of things change. We look at the world and
at people in a different way. Jesus encourages us to look at
life in the way he did. He was involved in humankind. We
need to be as well.*

> Love divine, all loves excelling,
> Joy of Heaven, to earth come down,
> Fix in us thy humble dwelling,
> All thy faithful mercies crown.
> Jesus, thou art all compassion,
> Pure, unbounded love thou art;
> Visit us with thy salvation,
> Enter every longing heart.
>
> Come, almighty to deliver,
> Let us all thy grace receive;
> Suddenly return, and never,
> Never more thy temples leave.
> Thee we would be always blessing,
> Serve thee as thy hosts above;
> Pray and praise thee without ceasing,
> Glory in thy perfect love.

Finish then thy new creation,
Pure and spotless let us be;
Let us see thy great salvation,
Perfectly restored in thee.
Changed from glory into glory,
Till in Heaven we take our place,
Till we cast our crowns before thee,
Lost in wonder, love and praise.

(*SASB* 438)

Personal Reflection

Dear Lord

It is a wonderful thing to be able to live in your light and your love in this world. Help us to look at the world in the way that you did. Help us not to be afraid to become involved with people. We need your compassion, your divine love to reach out to others. Amen.

Thursday – Change of direction

Bible readings: Isaiah 35:8-10; Matthew 7:13-14; John 10:27; John 12:26

'Enter through the narrow gate. For wide is the gate and broad is the road that leads to destruction, and many enter through it. But small is the gate and narrow the road that leads to life, and only a few find it' (Matthew 7:13-14).

When we become Christians we start to walk along the Way of Holiness. That means a change of direction in our lives as our plans and ambitions are put aside and we try to follow God's plans for our lives. For some of us it will mean a radical change – for others the change of direction will not be so noticeable to other people. But the change will have taken place.

> Jesus comes! Let all adore him!
> Lord of mercy, love and truth,
> Now prepare the way before him,
> Make the rugged places smooth;
> Through the desert mark his road,
> Make a highway for our God.
>
> Jesus comes! Reward is with him,
> Let the valleys all be raised,
> God's great glory now revealing
> As the mountains are abased.
> Lift thy voice and greet the Lord,
> Cry to Zion: See thy God!

Jesus comes! The Christ is marching
Through the places waste and wild;
He his Kingdom is enlarging
Where no verdure ever smiled.
Soon the desert will be glad
And with beauty shall be clad.

Jesus comes! Where thorns have flourished
Trees shall now be seen to grow,
Stablished by the Lord and nourished,
Strong and fair and fruitful too.
They shall rise on every side,
Spread their branches far and wide.

Jesus comes! From barren mountains
Rivers shall begin to flow,
There the Lord will open fountains
And supply the plains below;
As he passes, every land
Shall acclaim his powerful hand.

(*SASB* 159)

Personal Reflection

Dear Lord

We want to travel on the Way of Holiness. We can only set foot on it when we have given ourselves to you completely. When we do that, we see everything from a new perspective – our plans and ambitions no longer matter in the light of doing what you want us to. Give us the courage, Lord, to take that step. Amen.

Friday – Change of clothes

Bible readings: Psalm 30:11-12; Colossians 3:13-14; Ephesians 6:10-18

'You turned my wailing into dancing; you removed my sackcloth and clothed me with joy, that my heart may sing to you and not be silent. O Lord my God, I will give you thanks for ever' (Psalm 30:11-12).

Becoming a Christian means getting a whole new wardrobe. We have to make sure that we are properly dressed at all times. After all, people will be able to see what we are 'wearing'. But perhaps the most important part of the wardrobe is the armour we are issued with so we can help fight against the Devil's schemes.

> Soldiers of Christ, arise,
> And put your armour on,
> Strong in the strength which God supplies
> Through his eternal Son.
>
> Strong in the Lord of hosts,
> And in his mighty power,
> Who in the strength of Jesus trusts
> Is more than conqueror.
>
> Leave no unguarded place,
> No weakness of the soul;
> Take every virtue, every grace,
> And fortify the whole.

To keep your armour bright
Attend with constant care,
Still walking in your captain's sight
And watching unto prayer.

That, having all things done,
And all your conflicts past,
Ye may o'ercome through Christ alone,
And stand complete at last.

From strength to strength go on,
Wrestle and fight and pray;
Tread all the powers of darkness down,
And win the well-fought day.

(*SASB* 695)

Personal Reflection

Dear Lord

Please clothe us in what we need to wear in this world.
Help us to remember that we are all engaged in a spiritual
battle as Christians. We need that armour, Lord. But help us
to remember, too, that you clothe us with joy as we live our
lives for you. Thank you, Lord. Amen.

Saturday – 'Courage To Live' by Flora Larsson

LORD, give me the courage to live!
A cheerful courage, Master, if that might be.
Let me wear a smile even when my heart trembles;
let laughter-lines form round my eyes,
and let me hold my chin up
and go forward.

Lord, give me courage to live!
A grim, unsmiling courage, if need be.
>Courage to face the empty days,
>unfulfilled hopes,
>black hours,
>defeats, maybe;
a hard, defiant courage, that will hang on until things are
better.
>Grant me that, Lord.

Master, give me courage to live!
Your servant Sangster wrote that 'in the dark
>brave souls hold on to the skirts of God'.
Give me courage like that, Lord,
>clinging courage, desperate courage,
>that will not let you go.
If feeling goes, if faith goes, if fortitude fails,
>let me just hold on, clinging to you,
>knowing that you are there,
>counting on you to see me through.

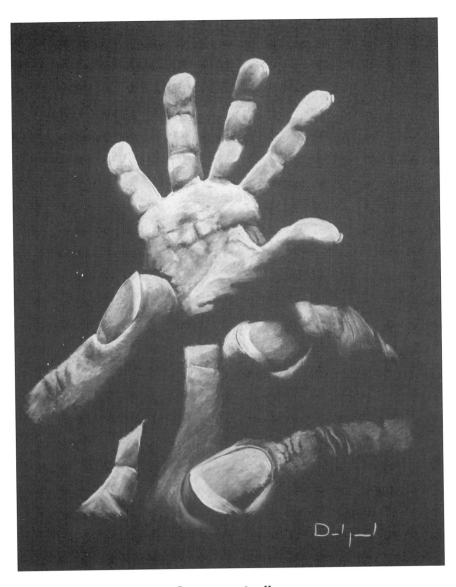

Courage to live

'A hard, defiant courage that will hang on'

Something To Do

Pray for countries where Christians are persecuted for their faith –where being a follower of Jesus poses a real threat. See if you can find out names of expatriate reinforcement officers serving in those countries and commit to praying for them every day this week.

4th Sunday – Opportunity In A Crisis

The word 'crisis' in Chinese is made up of two characters – those representing danger and opportunity.

There's no denying that for Jesus Gethsemane was a dangerous place. He could no longer escape the authorities who were hell-bent on his execution, for his considered choice to take his ministry into Jerusalem had made sure of it.

And when Jesus chose to go to Gethsemane to pray, he was fully aware that Judas knew exactly where to take the soldiers to arrest him (see John 18:1-3).

But Jesus' crisis in Gethsemane was also his opportunity to make an important choice that confirmed all his previous choices – a choice of that between good and better during his temptations in the desert; the choice to be the 'Suffering Servant' and not the conquering hero that the Jews were looking for; the choice to confront his enemies in their stronghold of Jerusalem.

Making decisions in a crisis is a lonely business. And Jesus discovered this again in Gethsemane. He could share the depths of his inner agony only with God. He felt that he could not face what lay ahead: 'Take this cup of suffering away from me' (Mark 14:36 *GNB*). But such was his trust in God's plan and purpose that he was able to add, 'Yet not what I want, but what you want.'

In Gethsemane Jesus accepted the fact that it was not possible to escape from the physical and mental suffering that awaited him. 'God is most emphatically not an escape … enabling us to evade the horrors and suffering of human life. Too often in the past God and religion have been presented as pain-killers, as though God were a magician who will melt our troubles away like snow in the sun, giving us a divine relief from the hard facts of the real world,' wrote H. A. Williams.

There was no escape for Jesus, neither was his spiritual pain and apprehension deadened. Even at his death he was to cry, 'My God, my God, why have you forsaken me?' (Mark 15:34 NIV).

But in choosing to face what menaced him from outside and tortured him within, Jesus won through to victory.

'It is unlikely that we shall ever have to go through an experience as deep and devastating as Christ's own in Gethsemane. But we may approach it, even if only from afar. God won't provide a magic escape. ...

'What God will enable us to do is face these unpleasant, ugly, disturbing, frightening, sometimes agonising facts and feelings. ... And as with Jesus, so with us; the acceptance will bring the victory' (H. A. Williams).

Gethsemane was also a special opportunity for some of the disciples, an opportunity which they missed. Jesus shared his turmoil with Peter, James and John: 'The sorrow in my heart is so great that it almost crushes me,' he confided (Mark 14:34 GNB). Then he asked for their support in his crisis: 'Stay here and keep watch.'

The disciples may have heard his words but they didn't listen to what he was saying. Had they really understood how very much he needed them at that moment, they certainly would not have slept, no matter how tired they were.

While they may not have been able to enter into his inner torment, it would have comforted Jesus simply to know that they were aware of the fact that he was facing a crisis and that they were supporting him in it with their presence.

The disciples were the losers. To have stood by Jesus, even without any action on their part, would have strengthened them, made them better men. John's Gospel records that when Peter did go to Jesus' aid, it was in the wrong way completely (see 18:10-11). He used violence, contrary to Jesus' teaching that he was to win victory through suffering and not by force.

Danger was the least important part of the crisis that Jesus and his disciples faced in Gethsemane, although it was very real. The options open to them and the choices that they made were far more significant.

For the disciples Gethsemane meant failure. But while Jesus may have spoken of a 'cup of suffering', his choice to do his Father-God's will transformed it into a chalice of opportunity.

Jean Bryant

Week Five

Monday – Consider your relationship with God

Bible readings: Genesis 1:27; Psalm 8:3-9; Matthew 6:9-10; John 14:8-10

'When I consider your heavens, the work of your fingers, the moon and the stars, which you have set in place, what is man that you are mindful of him, the son of man that you care for him?' (Psalm 8:3-4).

How do we think of God? Is he our Creator? Yes. Are we made in his image? Yes. Is he all-powerful, all-knowing, everywhere present? Yes. Is he a remote being totally divorced from his creation? No. Jesus came to show us that God is our heavenly Father and that we are his precious and dearly beloved children.

Eternal God, unchanging
Through all the changing years,
Whose hands all things created,
Who holds the countless stars;
Enthroned in heavenly glory,
Yet not a God afar;
Thou deignest to have dwelling
Here where thy people are.

Forbid that man's achievements
Should cause our faith to wane,
Or seek in human wisdom
Our spirit to sustain;
Lord, surely thou art shaping

All things to thy design,
And born of this conviction
Is faith to match our time.

And in a world divided
By selfishness and guile,
When truth is on the scaffold
And faith is standing trial,
Grant us, by inward knowledge
No learning can bestow,
A faith that answers firmly:
These things, these things I know.

Though men have wrought confusion
Thy hand still holds the plan,
And thou, at length, decidest
The destiny of man;
Dominions rise and perish,
The mighty have their day,
But still thy word abideth,
It shall not pass away.

(*SASB* 6)

Personal Reflection

Dear heavenly Father

Thank you so much that you are involved in your creation.
We can be assured that we are precious to you because we
are your children. We are a part of your plan and that is still
unfolding, in spite of what people do. Help us to follow you
closely as your plan unfolds. Amen.

Tuesday – Consider your relationship with Jesus

Bible readings: John 1:1-4; Matthew 16:13-16; John 6:35; John 11:25-26; John 14:6

'I am the way and the truth and the life. No one comes to the Father except through me' (John 14:6).

How do we think of Jesus? Do we see him as a great man, a wonderful teacher, a prophet, a healer? He was all these things. But the most important thing is for us to recognise him as our Saviour. He died on the cross so our sins could be forgiven. He wants to have a personal relationship with each of us. To have the life he promises, we must call him Saviour and Lord.

> Saviour of light, I look just now to thee;
> Brighten my path, so only shall I see
> Thy footprints, Lord, which mark the way for me;
> Light of my life, so surely thou wilt be,
> O Man of Galilee!
>
> *O Man of Galilee,*
> *Stay with and strengthen me;*
> *Walk thou through life with me,*
> *O Man of Galilee!*
>
> Another touch, I ask another still,
> That daily, hourly, I may do thy will;
> Healer of wounds and bearer of all pain,
> Thy touch, thy power are evermore the same,
> O Man of Galilee!

Lord of my life, I dare step out to thee
Who stilled the waves and stayed the tossing sea;
When floods o'erwhelm, my safety thou wilt be;
When nightfall comes, O Lord, abide with me;
O Man of Galilee!

Pilot of souls, I trust thy guiding hand;
Take thou the helm and, at thy blest command,
I sail straight on until, the harbour won,
I reach the glory of thy sweet well done;
O Man of Galilee!

(*SASB* 628)

Personal Reflection

Dear Lord Jesus

It is almost overwhelming, what you did and are doing for us. Your love for us took you to the cross. Your sacrifice means that we can be born again into the family of God. Thank you, Jesus. Help us to be worthy of what you did. Help us to live so that others will come to know you, too. Amen.

Wednesday – Consider your relationship with other people

Bible readings: Matthew 22:35-40; Matthew 9:35-38; 1 Corinthians 13:13

'"Love the Lord your God with all your heart and with all your soul and with all your mind." This is the first and greatest commandment. And the second is like it: "Love your neighbour as yourself." All the Law and the Prophets hang on these two commandments' (Matthew 22:37-40).

How do we view other people? Jesus tells us to love each other. Sometimes it isn't easy but Jesus wants us to reach out to others. We are his hands, his feet, his voice in this world. Jesus loves us and he will give us his love, grace and strength as we need these qualities.

The Saviour of men came to seek and to save
The souls who were lost to the good;
His Spirit was moved for the world which he loved
With the boundless compassion of God.
And still there are fields where the labourers are few,
And still there are souls without bread,
And still eyes that weep where the darkness is deep,
And still straying sheep to be led.

Except I am moved with compassion,
How dwelleth thy Spirit in me?
In word and in deed
Burning love is my need;
I know I can find this in thee.

O is not the Christ 'midst the crowd of today
Whose questioning cries do not cease?
And will he not show to the hearts that would know
The things that belong to their peace?
But how shall they hear if the preacher forbear
Or lack in compassionate zeal?
Or how shall hearts move with the Master's own love,
Without his anointing and seal?

It is not with might to establish the right,
Nor yet with the wise to give rest;
The mind cannot show what the heart longs to know
Nor comfort a people distressed.
O Saviour of men, touch my spirit again,
And grant that thy servant may be
Intense every day, as I labour and pray,
Both instant and constant for thee.

(*SASB* 527)

Personal Reflection

Dear Lord

You want us to reach out to others – and sometimes that is
difficult, we have to admit. Help us to see you in other
people, Lord. If we can do that then we can love them in
your name – even the most unlovable. Amen.

Thursday – Consider how you view the present

Bible readings: Psalm 23; Psalm 27:1, 4-5; John 16:33; Romans 8:38-39

'For I am convinced that neither death nor life, neither angels nor demons, neither the present nor the future, nor any powers, neither height nor depth, nor anything else in all creation, will be able to separate us from the love of God that is in Christ Jesus our Lord' (Romans 8:38-39).

How do we live our lives from day to day? Do we rejoice in the knowledge that God loves us and cares for us or are we overwhelmed by the awful things we see going on in the world? We can rest in God's love. There is nothing that can take us out of it.

> God's love is as high as the heavens,
> God's love is as deep as the sea,
> God's love is for all kinds of sinners,
> God's love is sufficient for me.
>
> *God's love, God's love,*
> *God's love is sufficient for me;*
> *God's love, God's love,*
> *God's love is sufficient for me.*
>
> God's love is as wide as creation,
> God's love is as boundless and free,
> God's love, it has brought my salvation,
> God's love is sufficient for me.

God's love brought his Son down from Heaven,
God's love let him die on the tree;
God's love, it can never be measured,
God's love is sufficient for me.

(*SASB* 47)

Personal Reflection

Dear Lord

We know, because your word tells us, that there is nothing that can take us out of your love. We also know that your love has no boundaries – there is no one who has to remain outside your love. Your love is enough for us – it is all we need to get on with the business of living. Thank you, Lord. Amen.

Friday – Consider how you view the future

Bible readings: Matthew 24:27-31; Philippians 2:9-11; John 14:1-4; Revelation 22:1-5

'Do not let your hearts be troubled. Trust in God; trust also in me. In my Father's house are many rooms; if it were not so, I would have told you. I am going there to prepare a place for you. And if I go and prepare a place for you, I will come back and take you to be with me that you also may be where I am. You know the way to the place where I am going' (John 14:1-4).

We have been given the promise of eternal life. It is a glorious thought. We may not know exactly what is going to happen or when but we can trust God that, as long as we have given our lives into his keeping in this world, we will be with him in the world which is to come.

When the trumpet of the Lord shall sound, and time shall be no more,
And the morning breaks, eternal, bright and fair,
When the saved of earth shall gather over on the other shore,
And the roll is called up yonder, I'll be there.

When the roll is called up yonder, I'll be there.

On that bright and cloudless morning, when the dead in Christ shall rise,
And the glory of his resurrection share,
When his chosen ones shall gather to their home beyond the skies,
And the roll is called up yonder, I'll be there.

Let us labour for the Master from the dawn till setting sun,
Let us tell of all his wondrous love and care;
Then, when all of life is over, and our work on earth is done,
And the roll is called up yonder, we'll be there.

(SASB 907)

Personal Reflection

Dear Lord

We can't see into the future but we know that you are there, just as you are here with us in the present. We know that we can trust you, Lord, whatever the future may hold. Just keep reminding us to keep our eyes firmly fixed on you. Amen.

Saturday – 'Faith' by John Gowans

There is a time for tears,
A time for sighing;
There is a place for grief,
A place for crying.
But in the mystery of
Unanswered prayers
Let faith hold fast to this:
God cares!

The sun won't always shine,
Sometimes the rain clouds form
And from the once-clear sky
May fall the thunderstorm.
The unexpected stress
Awakens sleeping fears,
And faith must find its way
Through mists of bitter tears.

It's easy to believe
In providential care
When faith is still untried
By doubt and black despair.
But in the longest night,
When fear and pain are real,
There faith will prove itself,
Its hidden strength reveal.

There is a time for tears,
A time for sighing;
There is a place for grief,
A place for crying.

But in the mystery of
Unanswered prayers
Let faith hold fast to this:
God cares!

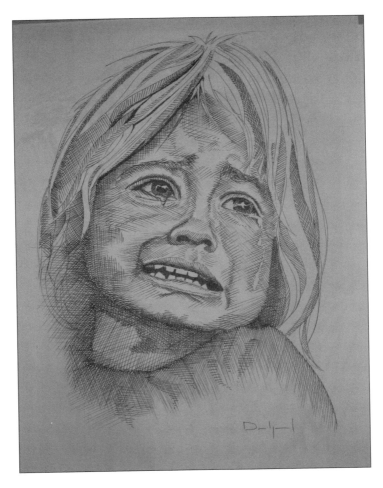

Faith

'There is a place for crying'

Something To Do

Write a letter to a friend you haven't been in touch with for a while. Catch up on news, wish him/her a blessed Easter and pray for him/her as you post it.

5th Sunday – Exerting Obedient Faith

Someone has said that obedience is 'the prime requisite for the Christian life'. If this is so we have to consider it carefully, not simply as an important principle for others, but as a requirement laid upon us all.

This is true even though obedience appears, at first thought, unpalatable. We are conditioned these days to words like 'independence', 'self-awareness' and 'self-determination', as well as 'consultation', 'discussion' and 'consensus'. Unquestioning obedience is not an up-to-date idea!

Of course, there are areas in which independence and consensus are wholly appropriate. Obedience to Christ does not take our thinking faculties from us and deprive us of a sense of personal responsibility. This is clearly not the case, since God made us thinking, rational, responsible beings.

Obedience is emphasised and strongly enjoined in Scripture. In the Garden of Eden story we see how the man and woman's fellowship with God was broken by their disobedience (Genesis 3:1-19).

In a later reference it is underlined that Israel would prosper only as long as she obeyed God in all things; disobedience would lead to disaster (Deuteronomy 28:1, 2, 15). In the chequered history of the Chosen People it did – more than once. This once led to the well-known question: 'Does the Lord delight in burnt offerings and sacrifices as much as in obeying the voice of the Lord? To obey is better than sacrifice …' (1 Samuel 15:22).

The importance of obedience is also underlined in the New Testament. In the familiar story of the great catch of fish (John 21:1-6), Jesus commanded his disciples, after their failure to land a catch, to let down their nets on the right side of the boat. Experienced fishermen, such as they undoubtedly were, might well have thought that their specialist knowledge would have enabled them to make the right decision themselves in such a matter. But they nevertheless obeyed, and their obedience led to success. Christ-directed service always will.

Later, in the great upper room discourses, Jesus told his disciples directly that only as they obeyed his commands would they remain in his love (John 14:15; 15:9, 10). The Scriptures are clear; the word is constant: God requires our obedience.

But, despite such unambiguous teaching, obedience does not come easily, even to those who sincerely want to follow Christ. Wrote J. S. Stewart: 'It is so very much easier to spend a dozen hours discussing religion, than one half-hour obeying God.' But without obedience, as we have seen, there can be no rewarding fellowship, no fruitful service.

Obedience is a mark of trusting in the one who gives the commands. So, even when the reason for God's demand is not clear – and sometimes it isn't – the disciple will nonetheless obey. He knows that God is concerned only with his children's good. 'Our obedience must go on,' wrote an experienced Christian counsellor, 'even when it seems to no purpose, even to Calvary.'

Many disappointments in spiritual life are traceable, not to lack of desire for grace or goodness; not to our unwillingness to give, in substance and in service, even to the point of sacrifice – but to our reluctance to obey.

Yet, in the words of Hannah Pearsall Smith, the 19th-century writer whose book, *The Christian's Secret Of A Happy Life*, contributed greatly to the establishing of the Keswick

Convention, 'Perfect obedience would be perfect happiness if only we had perfect confidence in the power we were obeying.' To which we might add, 'And perfect confidence in the love we were obeying.'

Obedience, as we have said, is not easy, though we often give the impression that we think it is and that we are more than willing for it. How easy it is for us to sing, 'Obey thee I will ever', 'Thee, only thee, resolved to obey', 'All my will conform to thine' – and so on.

Let us pray that, on the great day when we stand before Christ to give an account of our discipleship, we shall not be indicted for making all kinds of promises with our lips but not with our hearts.

It is only in the short term, however, that obedience to Christ may lead to loss and pain. In the end the result is true fulfilment. In one of his sermons, Leslie Weatherhead remarked that it is a pity that we reserve the words 'Thy will be done' for the tragedies of life and put the text so frequently on our tombstones! For, as one of our Army choruses has it, 'The *best* thing I know in this world below is doing the will of God.'

Is the idea of obedience, then, as unpalatable as we may have thought? Not when we know how greatly we are loved by the one who gives the commands. And not when we understand something of the purpose of what he asks of us – our growth in holiness and our joy in his love and peace.

These are indeed great truths to think about during this time of Lent, as we move forward to concentrated and grateful contemplation of him who obeyed, even to the cross (Philippians 2:8).

Will Clark

Week Six

Monday – Christ died for us

Bible readings: John 15:13; Romans 5:6-11; 1 Timothy 1:15

'Greater love has no one than this, that he lay down his life for his friends' (John 15:13).

Jesus loves us so much he was willing to die for us. He died to take the punishment for our sins upon himself. It is an incredible thought and, when we accept it, it will change our lives completely and for ever.

> When I survey the wondrous cross
> On which the Prince of Glory died,
> My richest gain I count but loss,
> And pour contempt on all my pride.
>
> Forbid it, Lord, that I should boast
> Save in the death of Christ, my God;
> All the vain things that charm me most,
> I sacrifice them to his blood.
>
> See, from his head, his hands, his feet,
> Sorrow and love flow mingled down;
> Did e'er such love and sorrow meet,
> Or thorns compose so rich a crown?
>
> Were the whole realm of nature mine,
> That were a present far too small;
> Love so amazing, so divine,
> Demands my soul, my life, my all.

(SASB 136)

Personal Reflection

Dear Jesus

You gave your life for us. That sacrifice demands our souls, our lives, our all. But as we surrender them to you, you make us into something incredible, you make us into citizens of the Kingdom of God. Whatever we give to you, it is nothing compared to all you give to us day by day. Thank you, Lord. Amen.

Tuesday – Christ lives in us

Bible readings: John 15:4-8; John 17:25-26; Galatians 2:20; Matthew 28:20

'I have been crucified with Christ and I no longer live, but Christ lives in me. The life I live in the body, I live by faith in the Son of God, who loved me and gave himself for me' (Galatians 2:20).

There is never a moment when we need to feel separated from Jesus. Sometimes we do, but that isn't because Jesus has moved away – it's because we have. We can reach out and feel his presence even when the world is at its darkest.

> It's no longer I that liveth,
> But Christ that liveth in me,
> It's no longer I that liveth,
> But Christ that liveth in me.
> He lives! He lives!
> Jesus is alive in me.
> It's no longer I that liveth,
> But Christ that liveth in me.

(*SASB* Chorus Section 177)

Personal Reflection

Dear Jesus

When we give our lives into your keeping you actually take up residence within us. We become temples of the living Lord! Help us to keep those temples fit places for you to be. And may we never do anything that would cause anyone else to think less of you. Amen.

Wednesday – Christ promises us eternal life

Bible readings: John 3:16; Romans 6:5-14; Romans 6:23

'For God so loved the world that he gave his one and only Son, that whoever believes in him shall not perish but have eternal life' (John 3:16).

Following Jesus means that our relationship with him will never end. Because of what he did for us on the cross, we can claim this amazing promise of eternal life.

O joyful sound! O glorious hour
When Christ by his almighty power
Arose and left the grave!
Now let our songs his triumph tell
Who broke the chains of death and Hell,
And ever lives to save.

*He lives, he lives,
I know that my redeemer lives.*

The first-begotten of the dead,
For us he rose, our glorious head,
Immortal life to bring.
What though the saints like him shall die,
They share their leader's victory,
And triumph with their King.

No more we tremble at the grave;
For he who died our souls to save
Will raise our bodies too.
What though this earthly house shall fail,
The Saviour's power will yet prevail
And build it up anew.

(SASB 149)

Personal Reflection

Dear Jesus

How wonderful to think that our lives with you will never end. You have given us the assurance of eternal life that will mean that we will dwell in the presence of God for ever. How can we thank you enough for that? Amen.

Thursday – Christ loves us

Bible readings: John 15:9-13; Romans 8:35-39; Ephesians 5:1-2

'As the Father has loved me, so have I loved you. Now remain in my love. If you obey my commands, you will remain in my love, just as I have obeyed my Father's commands and remain in his love. I have told you this so that my joy may be in you and that your joy may be complete. My command is this: Love each other as I have loved you' (John 15:9-12).

It is wonderful to think how much Jesus loves us! But knowing that love in our lives means that we have to pass it on. We want other people to come to know Jesus because of the love we show.

> Loved with everlasting love,
> Led by grace that love to know;
> Spirit, breathing from above,
> Thou hast taught me this is so.
> O this full and perfect peace!
> O this transport all divine!
> In a love which cannot cease
> I am his and he is mine.

Heaven above is softer blue,
Earth around is sweeter green;
Something lives in every hue,
Christless eyes have never seen;
Birds with gladder songs o'erflow,
Flowers with deeper beauties shine,
Since I know, as now I know,
I am his and he is mine.

His for ever, only his;
Who the Lord and me shall part?
Ah! with what a rest of bliss
Christ can fill the loving heart.
Heaven and earth may fade and flee,
First-born light in gloom decline,
But, throughout eternity,
I am his and he is mine.

(SASB 545)

Personal Reflection

Dear Lord

Your love for us changes our lives and the way we see the world. When we realise just what that love means we live our lives in a completely different way. Help us, Lord, to show others what your love can do in their lives. Amen.

Friday – Christ is the Alpha and the Omega

Bible readings: Revelation 22:12-14; John 1:1-5; Revelation 22:20-21

'Behold, I am coming soon! My reward is with me, and I will give to everyone according to what he has done. I am the Alpha and the Omega, the First and the Last, the Beginning and the End' (Revelation 22:12-13).

There will come a time when Jesus returns in glory and the world as we know it will come to an end. But it won't really be the end – it will be a glorious new beginning!

Marching on in the light of God,
Marching on, I am marching on;
Up the path that the Master trod,
Marching, marching on.

A robe of white, a crown of gold,
A harp, a home, a mansion fair,
A victor's palm, a joy untold,
Are mine when I get there.
For Jesus is my Saviour, he's washed my sins away,
Died for me on Calvary's mountain;
I'm happy in his wondrous love, singing all the day,
I'm living, yes, I'm living in the fountain.

Marching on through the hosts of sin,
Marching on, I am marching on;
Victory's mine while I've Christ within;
Marching, marching on.

Marching on in the Spirit's might,
Marching on, I am marching on;
More than conqueror in every fight;
Marching, marching on.

Marching on with the flag unfurled,
Marching on, I am marching on;
Preaching Christ to a dying world;
Marching, marching on.

(SASB 811)

Personal Reflection

Dear Lord Jesus

Although we know you are the Alpha and Omega, the Beginning and the End – we also know that with you there is no end. When you come again in all your glory, it will mean a whole new beginning for those who follow you. Lord, as we wait for that moment keep us faithful in telling others about you. Amen.

Saturday – 'When God Expressed Himself'
by John Gowans

When God expressed himself
The Word he spoke
Was clearly understood
By ordinary folk.
They looked into his eyes,
One single looked sufficed;
Men read the mind of God
In the face of Christ.

When Christ laid down his head
Upon a manger bed,
His coming simply said:
God is with man!
Kneeling upon the hay,
We hear the Baby say:
Your God is here to stay;
God is with man!

When Christ was crucified
And hung his head and died,
His silenced body cried:
God loves like this!
And still to us today
Two thousand years away,
His suff'rings simply say:
God loves like this!

Something To Do

Take two kinds of walk – if possible. Go out into the countryside and thank God for the world he created. Then walk down a residential street and pray for the people in the houses you pass. Jesus died for every one of those people.

When God expressed himself

'In the face of Christ'

6th Sunday – Centring On The Cross

The cross was central to the ministry of our Lord: the prominence given to it in the New Testament testifies to that. It is the pivot of the salvation story, the event to which, through the ages, men and women have been drawn as if by a magnet and where they have wondered and worshipped, felt their sins forgiven and found their lives transformed.

All this is the focus of our thoughts in this meditation.

The Scriptures declare that Christ died for us – for our sins. The references are many: Matthew 2:28 and 26:28; Romans 5:6, 8 and 14:15; 1 Corinthians 8:11 and 15:3; 1 Thessalonians 4:14 and 5:10 and so on.

Throughout the centuries men have put forward various so-called theories of the atonement, each of which has been an attempt to explain how the cross 'works' for us. The songs in the 'Atoning Work' section of our songbook are worth a careful study in this connection. They show how the various writers have seen and interpreted the cross.

We find highlighted there what are referred to as the 'ransom' theories, in which Christ is seen as paying or becoming a ransom for the world. Jesus used the word of himself (Matthew 20:28). And the songbook example, among many, is song 114: 'Jesus came down my ransom to be'. Then there are those theories that see Christ as making a sacrifice for sin and rendering the Old Testament practice of animal sacrifice no longer necessary (song 120).

Then the cross is seen as a revelation of the love of God which draws men and women towards him in wonder and gratitude. The song, 'When I survey the wondrous cross' (136), is a classic statement of this idea. The song says nothing of sacrifice or ransom: only of God's love touching the heart of the one who 'surveys' the 'wondrous cross', constraining the person to love and to worship.

All these theories say something important and preserve some facet of a many-faceted truth; none of them says – or could say – everything on the subject, and the Church in its wisdom has never sanctioned one theory above another. It is the cross itself and not theories about it that saves. It means more than ransom, though the ransom aspect is valid. It means more than sacrifice, though without doubt sacrifice does come into it. It achieves something important in relation to the sins of humankind; it brings a new situation in which the penitent sinner may be forgiven and become a new creature in Christ Jesus.

There is yet another theory of the atonement which sees Christ on the cross battling with evil and winning a stupendous victory. Song 121, verse 5, and song 107, verse 4, both echo this profound truth.

This is particularly meaningful today, faced as we are with so much despair, fear and pessimism. The truth of the victorious Christ gets near to the heart of the matter. The cross must not be seen as a tragedy which the resurrection reversed. It was itself a triumph. Christ must not be seen as a victim of men's evil designs, though, as James S. Stewart pointed out, religious, political and social forces conspired to crucify the Son of God. Christ was victor, gloriously conquering the forces of evil. That needs to be said again and again.

But then, of course, on page after page the Gospels show a Christ victorious throughout his ministry. He was victor over demons – read for example Mark 1:23-27 and 34; he was victor over disease – Mark 1:32, 33 and many other places; he was victor over death – the death of others, Luke 7, Luke 8 and John 11. And he was, supremely, victor over his own death.

Then notice how, with the cross just around the corner, he held out a glorious promise for the future (Luke 22:29, 30). He spoke of his coming Kingdom which the disciples – to whom he was speaking – would share. Those were not the words of one facing defeat! Notice also the composure of Jesus in those last days and hours. In John's account of the trial before Pilate this is most marked (John 18:28 to 19:16). It is Jesus who is so obviously in control; Pilate almost seems to be the one on trial! A meek, submissive, vulnerable Jesus? From one angle, yes. But more importantly, and more truly, he was composed, strong and, even then, victorious.

When he spoke his last word from the cross it was a triumphant word: 'It is finished!' – that is, the work he had come to do was completed, accomplished. He was the perfect victor.

What does all this say to us now? Listen to Paul: 'Thanks be to God who gives us the victory through our Lord Jesus Christ' (1 Corinthians 15:57 *GNB*). Note carefully: 'Who gives *us* the victory.' We may share his victory: through him we too may triumph.

We may have victory over our fear, even now in our fear-filled world. We may have victory over our doubts, those doubts that question the sufficiency of his grace for our deepest needs. And we may have victory over our sins. Sin is the ultimate human problem, the malady at the heart of life. But by his cross Christ has conquered sin. The battle between love and evil was joined at Calvary and 'victory remains with love'. Praise God!

We shall never plumb the depths of the meaning of the cross. Yet, 'surpassing my reason', as Albert Orsborn wrote, it is nevertheless capable of 'winning my heart'.

In these days of Lent, as we think again of Christ of the cross, let us rejoice over the victory of Calvary. And rejoicing for ourselves, let us also determine to share the truth with others, so that in God's good time, and according to his sovereign purpose, the world may 'taste and see the riches of his grace'.

Will Clark

Holy Week

Monday – The cleansing of the Temple

Bible reading: Matthew 21:12-17

'Jesus entered the temple area and drove out all who were buying and selling there' (Matthew 21:12).

Jesus was angry at the way unscrupulous people were exploiting the pilgrims and those seeking to fulfil their religious duties. The Temple should have been a place of holiness and prayer, a place where God's will could be seen to be done. It wasn't. Jesus had set his feet upon the path leading to the cross when he entered Jerusalem on Palm Sunday. Now he takes another step on this journey as he cleanses the Temple and heals the blind and the lame.

> I would be thy holy temple,
> Sacred and indwelt by thee;
> Naught then could stain my commission,
> 'Tis thy divine charge to me.
>
> *Take thou my life, Lord,*
> *In deep submission I pray,*
> *My all to thee dedicating,*
> *Accept my offering today.*
>
> Seeking to mirror thy glory,
> Living to answer thy call,
> Each faithful vow now renewing,
> Gladly I yield thee my all.

Time, health and talents presenting,
All that I have shall be thine;
Heart, mind and will consecrating,
No longer shall they be mine.

O for a heart of compassion,
Moved at the impulse of love,
Lost ones to bring to thy footstool,
Thy gracious riches to prove!

(*SASB* 786)

Personal Reflection

Dear Lord

Help me to be angry over the right things. When I see injustice, cruelty or discrimination, give me the courage to stand up for what is right. Sometimes I might be tempted to sit quietly in a corner – but there are times when I need to stand up and be counted. Help be counted in your cause. Amen.

Tuesday – The authority of Jesus questioned

Bible reading: Matthew 21:23-27

'Jesus entered the temple courts, and, while he was teaching, the chief priests and the elders of the people came to him' (Matthew 21:23).

The chief priests and the elders were looking for a way to trap Jesus but he wasn't about to let them get him. In the same way he turned the tables over in the Temple, he turned the tables on his persecutors. They found themselves trapped between a rock and a hard place as they realised that whatever answer they gave to Jesus' question, it would be the wrong one.

> Thy Kingdom come, O God!
> Thy rule, O Christ, begin!
> Break with thine iron rod
> The tyrannies of sin.
>
> Where is thy reign of peace,
> And purity and love?
> When shall all hatred cease
> As in the realms above?
>
> When comes the promised time
> That war shall be no more,
> And lust, oppression, crime,
> Shall flee thy face before?

We pray thee, Lord, arise,
And come in thy great might;
Revive our longing eyes,
Which languish for thy sight.

Men scorn thy sacred name,
And wolves devour thy fold;
By many deeds of shame
We learn that love grows cold.

O'er lands both near and far
Thick darkness broodeth yet:
Arise, O morning star,
Arise, and never set!

(*KS* 89)

Personal Reflection

Dear Lord

Your authority is absolute – it is Kingdom authority. We pray to our Father so often, 'Your will be done on earth as it is in Heaven', and sometimes it is very difficult to see that his will is being done. But it can begin in us. May we be a place on earth where people can see that your will is being sought and followed. Amen.

Wednesday – A beautiful thing and betrayal

Bible reading: Matthew 26:6-16

'While Jesus was in Bethany in the home of a man known as Simon the Leper, a woman came to him with an alabaster jar of very expensive perfume, which she poured on his head as he was reclining at the table' (Matthew 26:6-7).

A beautiful action is followed by an act of betrayal. John actually says that Judas, as keeper of the money bag, was the one who complained about the wasteful use of the perfume. But in Jesus' eyes, the gift was infinitely precious and eternally memorable. However, it seems to be the catalyst which drives Judas to seek out the chief priests with his offer – to hand Jesus over to them.

> And is it so? A gift from me
> Dost thou, dear Lord, request?
> Then speak thy will, whate'er it be:
> Obeying, I am blest.
>
> *I have not much to give thee, Lord,*
> *For that great love which made thee mine:*
> *I have not much to give thee, Lord,*
> *But all I have is thine.*
>
> And dost thou ask a gift from me:
> The talents I possess?
> Such as I have I give to thee
> That others I may bless.

And dost thou ask a gift from me:
The gift of passing time?
My hours I'll give, not grudgingly,
I feel by right they're thine.

And dost thou ask a gift from me:
A loving, faithful heart?
'Tis thine, for thou on Calvary
For me with all didst part.

(SASB 475)

Personal Reflection

Dear Lord

We know that we don't have much to give you – especially when we look at all you have given to us. But what you really want from us is open, loving hearts and a willingness to seek your will for our lives. Help us to be what you want us to be, dear Jesus. Amen.

Thursday – The Last Supper

Bible reading: John 13:3-17

'Now that I, your Lord and Teacher, have washed your feet, you also should wash one another's feet. I have set you an example that you should do as I have done for you' (John 13:14-15).

The message could scarcely be clearer – we are to be the servants of our Servant Lord. Jesus tells us that we will be blessed if we follow his example in the way we serve others.

> I believe that God the Father
> Can be seen in God the Son,
> In the gentleness of Jesus
> Love for all the world is shown.
> Though men crucify their Saviour,
> And his tenderness rebuff,
> God is love, the cross is saying,
> Calvary is proof enough.
>
> I believe in transformation,
> God can change the hearts of men,
> And refine the evil nature
> Till it glows with grace again.
> Others may reject the weakling,
> I believe he can be strong,
> To the family of Jesus
> All God's children may belong.

In a world of shifting values,
There are standards that remain,
I believe that holy living
By God's grace we may attain.
All would hear the Holy Spirit
If they listen to his voice,
Every Christian may be Christlike
And in liberty rejoice.

All the promises of Jesus
Are unchanged in every way,
In my yesterdays I proved them,
I believe them for today.
Still God gives his willing servant
Full equipment for the task;
Power is found by those who seek it,
Grace is given to those who ask.

(*SASB* 324)

Personal Reflection

Dear Lord

Help me to have a servant's heart and be willing to reach out to others, whatever their needs are. Help me not to be too proud to serve. If you could wash your disciples' feet, Lord, I should be able to do whatever you ask of me. Amen.

Friday – Crucified

Bible reading: Mark 15:25-39

'It was the third hour when they crucified him' (Mark 15:25).

As we read about the Crucifixion, let us remember that Jesus went through it all for us.

> Behold him now on yonder tree,
> The Prince of Peace, the heavenly King;
> O what can his transgression be
> Such shameful punishment to bring?
> And lo, a thief hangs on each side;
> Who justly suffers for his crime.
> But why should Christ be crucified,
> The one so holy, so divine?
>
> *It was for me, yes, even me,*
> *That Jesus died on Calvary;*
> *My soul to cleanse from all its guilt,*
> *His precious blood my Saviour spilt.*
>
> O sinner, see, for you and me
> He freely suffers in our stead;
> And lo, he dies upon the tree;
> Behold, he bows his sacred head!
> So pure, yet he has borne our guilt,
> By death our ransom he has paid;
> It was for us his blood was spilt;
> Our every sin on him was laid.

O loving Saviour, take my heart,
No longer can I live from thee!
With all unlike thee now I part;
Thy wondrous love has conquered me.
I yield to thee my little all;
Accept me now, Lord, as thine own;
I'll be obedient to thy call
And spend my life for thee alone.

(*SASB* 108)

Personal Reflection

Dear Jesus

You died for me. I can hardly take it in. Help me to be
worthy of your sacrifice, Lord. Amen.

Saturday – 'Once, On A Day' by Albert Orsborn

Once, on a day, was Christ led forth to die,
And with the crowd that pressed on him joined I.
Slowly they led him, led him to the tree,
And I beheld his hands no more were free.
Bound fast with cords, and this was his distress,
That men denied those hands outstretched to bless.

Sacred hands of Jesus, they were bound for me;
Wounded hands of Jesus, stretched upon a tree,
Ever interceding, mercy is their plea.
Their effectual pleading brings grace to me,
Redeeming grace to me.

Hands that were scarred by daily fret and tear;
Hands quick to soothe the troubled brow of care;
Hands strong to smite the sins that men enthrone,
Yet never raised to seek or claim their own:
Dear hands of Christ! and yet men feared them so
That they must bind them as to death they go.

Hands that still break to men the living bread;
Hands full of power to raise again the dead,
Potent and healing, eager to reclaim,
Laid in forgiveness on one bowed in shame;
Say, wouldst thou bind, by pride and unbelief,
Those hands that compass all thy soul's relief?

(*SASB* 129)

Something To Do

Try your hand at making an Easter garden.

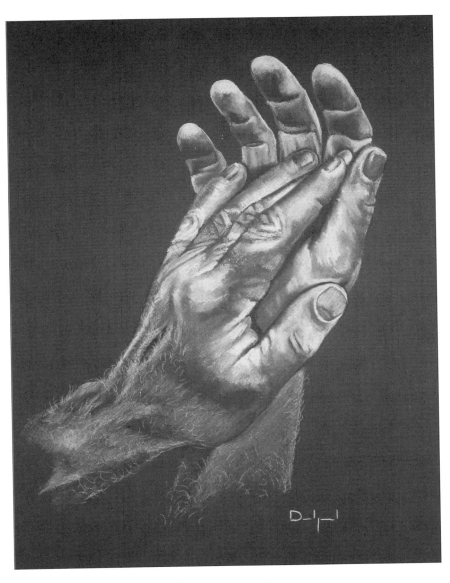

Once, on a day

'Their effectual pleading brings grace to me'

Easter Sunday – He Is Not Here!

The empty tomb is the central reason for our Easter celebrations. Its vacancy shook the people who made their way through the garden to the place where the Christ had been buried – and it shakes us still. It all seems too good to be true.

We need to be reminded that Christ did not burst his way through the roughly shaped circular stone door, smashing it to smithereens. He just was not there!

The angel did not roll away the stone to let him 'out'. Not at all. He had been 'in' but he wasn't 'in' any more and that was that!

The account tells us that the angel rolled back the stone and sat upon it with a kind of cheerful insolence. 'He's not here!' said the divine messenger. 'Have a look!' It seemed important that the world should see just how empty the place was.

The message must have become crystal-clear to his staggered disciples. The Master whom they thought was done for was up and about again – as ready as ever to comfort, to guide, to direct and correct, to help and to heal.

Love was liberated. The rocky walls of his 'container' could not contain him. What can one say but 'Whoopee!' or, perhaps more appropriately, 'Hallelujah!'

Our world needs to know about this. Every Christian ought to stand by the door of Christ's empty tomb and whisper or shout as may be appropriate: 'He is not here!'

Ever since the Christ moved out of his grave, people have been trying to get him back inside. They have attempted to imprison him afresh – in history, in literature, in tradition – but in each case the cry rings out: 'He isn't here!'

They try to wrap him up in the shroud of regimented religion, and the angels must laugh as they sing out, 'He isn't here either!'

Regular attempts have been made to bury him in the past but he is more modern than the latest revelation of man's way-out technology. Don't look for him among dead things. You won't find him there.

'Then where is he?' you ask. The simple answer is, 'Everywhere!' His presence is totally unrestricted, as his disciples soon found out.

He seemed to be everywhere at once and he still is. He is here with the fellow setting out for university and the girl going to her first job. He is here with the new mother cuddling her contented child. He is at the bedside of the seriously ill and on the road beside the recently redundant. He is here with the laughing crowd at the football match and at the Olympic Games. He is here with the lonely and the depressed and especially the bereaved, and a simple prayer will make this living, powerful presence felt.

He is the Christ of the human road. That's why we wish each other 'Happy Easter!'

John Gowans

Advent

1st Sunday – Jesus, Son Of David

There is a passage in Matthew's Gospel in which Jesus challenges the Pharisees: "'What do you think about the Christ? Whose son is he?" "The son of David," they replied' (22:42).

Mark and Luke report the difficult teaching which follows, but the opening question is particularly important to Matthew. To him the story of Jesus is the story of the son of David. This title appears in the first verse of the Gospel and makes frequent appearances in the telling of the story.

It seems that 'son of David' was a popular title for the expected Messiah and, as such, was an expression of hope.

King David's colourful lifestyle is well chronicled in the Old Testament, but so also is the catalogue of his achievements as a ruler. David gave his people political unity, peace and stability. His leadership led to the establishment of a capital in Jerusalem – a fit home for the Ark and the Tabernacle, symbols of God's presence with Israel – and the centre of true worship for the whole nation.

When Jesus is described as 'son of David' it is because he fulfils all the hope that the name 'David' invokes and serves as a remembrance that God has made promises to his people. After David's death the hard-won unity of the nation was lost, mainly due to Solomon's political ineptitude. The purity of worship that David had established was also lost, to be retrieved only spasmodically, and the boundaries of his kingdom were steadily eroded.

However, Israel never forgot his achievements and David's name was forever linked with Israel at her best – politically, socially, in terms of faith and, despite the scandals, even morally.

Psalm 132 records a promise made to David by God: 'One of your own descendants I will place on your throne' (v 11).

In the dark days of Israel, when Isaiah and Jeremiah prophesied doom to their respective generations, the remembrance of this promise gave some small light of hope. As the centuries rolled on, unfolding a story of national defeat and rebuilding, the hope that God would intervene on behalf of his people grew.

With this hope came also the expectation of a descendant of David who would embody this work of material restoration. By the time of Christ the hope and the expectations were at something near fever pitch. Since hopes tend to recede with time it says much for the tenacity and faith of the Jews that they kept the hope alive and growing for centuries.

George MacDonald wrote a Christmas carol which says, 'They all were looking for a king'. Indeed, some Jews *were* looking for a king, others had another kind of Messiah in mind.

It would be wrong to say that the Jews of Jesus' day were all expecting or hoping for the same thing, but at least they were united in their hope. Jesus is the centre of hope for his Church, despite the differences of emphasis among us. We are united in hope through Christ, even if we have never achieved unanimity. We are all looking for God to act – even though we might be looking for different kinds of action!

One of the most positive aspects of the Church Growth movement is that it has united people in a simple aspiration. What the language and theory of war did for us in the late

19th century, we hope that the language and theory of growth will do for the Church in Europe and America in the 21st century.

At the heart of growth teaching is the hope that God will act through what we feel he has initiated. It is the sense of expectation that gives the whole movement staying power.

To some Jews the son of David was the symbol of the hope of a return to political independence and greatness; to others he brought hope of a return to national faith and the practice of pure religion. The realistic Christian sees sense in the teaching that numerical strength and its attendant influence is only half the story. It is just as important to build on a foundation of sound faith and right living.

For Christians in the developing countries the name of Jesus represents the right of freedom from economic and racial oppression, based on a new awareness of each person's dignity and value as someone 'for whom Christ died'. To Christians in other parts of Europe and Asia recent years have brought a new freedom to worship. God is working to honour the longings of those who have remained faithful in the face of hostility. The son of David has become the centre of the deep and diverse inner longings of his beleaguered Church and God is acting in its midst. Despite the diverse aspirations of his people, God is still at work.

Strangely, in the Gospels the title 'son of David', with all its nationalist overtones, is most often heard from the lips of the poor and sick who pressed their claim on Jesus' time and power: blind Bartimaeus, the mother of a demon-possessed girl, the folk who witnessed the healing of a blind deaf-mute. Jesus represented for them a hope quite different in scale, but no different in principle, from the national hope.

They wanted God to intervene in their lives, to put things right for them, and Jesus was the means of that intervention. It takes courage to keep hope alive, and sometimes even more courage to allow it to be realised for us. But for these folk it was hope that gave them courage to ask for help from David's son.

Advent is a season of anticipation. May it be that all hearts find their hope in the son of David and that, when he comes to us, we'll be ready to accept the new and unexpected thing he wants to accomplish in us. May we also learn to accept what he is doing for others whose lives are a closed book to us.

On TV a few years ago a young man spoke of returning to Northern Ireland following a trip to India. He'd always thought he had an understanding of the situation in Ulster, and of the aspirations of the separated communities in that province. India, with its poverty and disease, had taught him a simple lesson: the world was bigger than he'd thought, its problems more immediate and serious than those he'd grown up with.

It's not a bad lesson for any of us to learn, nor is the corresponding lesson that God has more on his plate than the sorting out of our immediate situation. Many Jews made the mistake of seeing their hope only in terms of limited action in support of their own cause. When the son of David did appear it was to bless and save all of humankind.

It's sometimes hard to accept when God does something more than we expected and moves in his mysterious way in places we'd never thought of.

Ian Barr

Monday – To us a child is born

Bible readings: Isaiah 9:2-7; John 1:1-9

'The people walking in darkness have seen a great light; on those living in the land of the shadow of death a light has dawned' (Isaiah 9:2).

Long before Christ was born, Isaiah prophesied about what would happen. The years of darkness would come to an end when Jesus came to this world to be its light.

> A light came out of darkness;
> No light, no hope had we,
> Till Jesus came from Heaven
> Our light and hope to be.
> Oh, as I read the story
> From birth to dying cry,
> A longing fills my bosom
> To meet him by and by.
>
> *Shall you, shall I, meet Jesus by and by?*
> *And when we reach the Glory land,*
> *We'll swell the song of the angel band.*
> *Shall you, shall I, meet Jesus by and by?*
>
> How tender his compassion,
> How loving was his call,
> How earnest his entreaty
> To sinners, one and all.
> He wooed and won them to him
> By love, and that is why
> I long to be like Jesus,
> And meet him by and by.

Yet deeper do I ponder,
His cross and sorrow see,
And ever gaze and wonder
Why Jesus died for me.
And shall I fear to own him?
Can I my Lord deny?
No! let me love him, serve him,
And meet him by and by.

(*SASB* 94)

Personal Reflection

Dear Lord

We thank you that you came to be this world's light. It seems as if people are still walking in darkness, still living in a land of shadows. But your light has never grown dim. As we begin to prepare ourselves for Christmas, help us to focus on your brightness. Amen.

Tuesday – Immanuel, God with us

Bible readings: Isaiah 7:13-14; Matthew 1:18-25

'Then Isaiah said: "Hear, now, you house of David! Is it not enough to try the patience of men? Will you try the patience of my God also? Therefore the Lord himself will give you a sign: The virgin will be with child and will give birth to a son, and will call him Immanuel"' (Isaiah 7:13-14).

Immanuel. God with us. What an amazing thought! God enters his creation as a human being to save people from their sins. Jesus came to be with us and has never left us. An awareness of his presence is very precious to those who believe.

> Hark! the herald angels sing:
> Glory to the new-born King;
> Peace on earth, and mercy mild,
> God and sinners reconciled.
> Joyful, all ye nations rise,
> Join the triumph of the skies;
> With the angelic host proclaim,
> Christ is born in Bethlehem.
>
> *Hark! the herald angels sing:*
> *Glory to the new-born King.*

Christ, by highest Heaven adored,
Christ, the everlasting Lord,
Late in time behold him come,
Offspring of a virgin's womb.
Veiled in flesh the Godhead see;
Hail the incarnate Deity!
Pleased as man with man to dwell,
Jesus, our Immanuel.

Hail the Heaven-born Prince of Peace!
Hail the Sun of righteousness!
Light and life to all he brings,
Risen with healing in his wings.
Mild he lays his glory by,
Born that man no more may die,
Born to raise the sons of earth,
Born to give them second birth.

(*SASB* 82)

Personal Reflection

Dear Lord

Thank you that you came to be with us and you have never left us. You are Immanuel – God with us. When we reach out you are there. There is nothing that can separate us from your love for us. Thank you for the strength and comfort that assurance brings. Amen.

Wednesday – A promised ruler from Bethlehem

Bible readings: Micah 5:2-5; Luke 2:1-7

'But you, Bethlehem Ephrathah, though you are small among the clans of Judah, out of you will come for me one who will be ruler over Israel, whose origins are from of old, from ancient times' (Micah 5:2).

Joseph lived in Nazareth but he belonged to the house and line of David, so he had to go to Bethlehem at the time of the census. Micah had prophesied about 700 years earlier that Bethlehem would be the birthplace of the Messiah. It is an amazing thought how many things fell into place so that Jesus' birth would happen as planned.

O little town of Bethlehem,
How still we see thee lie!
Above thy deep and dreamless sleep
The silent stars go by.
Yet in thy dark streets shineth
The everlasting light;
The hopes and fears of all the years
Are met in thee tonight.

O morning stars, together
Proclaim the holy birth,
And praises sing to God, the King,
And peace to men on earth.
For Christ is born of Mary;
And, gathered all above,
While mortals sleep, the angels keep
Their watch of wondering love.

How silently, how silently
The wondrous gift is given!
So God imparts to human hearts
The blessings of his Heaven.
No ear may hear his coming;
But in this world of sin,
Where meek souls will receive him, still
The dear Christ enters in.

O holy Child of Bethlehem,
Descend to us, we pray;
Cast out our sin, and enter in,
Be born in us today.
We hear the Christmas angels
The great glad tidings tell;
O come to us, abide with us,
Our Lord Immanuel.

(*SASB* 86)

Personal Reflection

Dear Father God

We can scarcely even begin to grasp the amount of planning that went into Jesus' birth. And how amazing it is that we can read prophecies in the Old Testament which Jesus came to fulfil! Thank you for all you did and are still doing for us. Thank you for your wonderful love. Amen.

Thursday – A throne established for ever

Bible readings: 2 Samuel 7:11-16; Luke 1:26-33

'Do not be afraid, Mary, you have found favour with God. You will be with child and give birth to a son, and you are to give him the name Jesus. He will be great and will be called the Son of the Most High. The Lord God will give him the throne of his father David, and he will reign over the house of Jacob for ever; his kingdom will never end' (Luke 1:30-33).

David was considered a great king. God gave him the wonderful assurance that his throne would be established for ever. David might have thought that it meant that his descendants would remain on the throne – but it had an eternal meaning, too. From David's line would come the Messiah, whose Kingdom would know no end.

> Crown him with many crowns,
> The Lamb upon his throne;
> Hark! how the heavenly anthem drowns
> All music but its own;
> Awake, my soul, and sing
> Of him who died for thee,
> And hail him as thy matchless King
> Through all eternity.
>
> Crown him the Lord of life,
> Who triumphed o'er the grave,
> And rose victorious in the strife
> For those he came to save;
> His glories now we sing

Who died, and rose on high,
Who died eternal life to bring,
And lives, that death may die.

Crown him the Lord of peace,
Whose power a sceptre sways
From pole to pole, that wars may cease
And all be prayer and praise;
His reign shall know no end,
And round his piercèd feet
Fair flowers of Paradise extend
Their fragrance ever sweet.

Crown him the Lord of love;
Behold his hands and side.
Those wounds, yet visible above,
In beauty glorified;
All hail, redeemer, hail!
For thou hast died for me;
Thy praise and glory shall not fail
Throughout eternity.

(*SASB* 156)

Personal Reflection

Dear Lord

When we give our lives to you it isn't just for the here and now but it is for all eternity. Your Kingdom will never end and, when we become part of your family, we become part of your Kingdom. Thank you that we have the promise of eternal life with you. Amen.

Friday – A Branch from Jesse

Bible readings: Isaiah 11:1-10; Luke 1:68-79

'A shoot will come up from the stump of Jesse; from his roots a Branch will bear fruit. The Spirit of the Lord will rest on him – the Spirit of wisdom and of understanding, the Spirit of counsel and of power, the Spirit of knowledge and of the fear of the Lord – and he will delight in the fear of the Lord' (Isaiah 11:1-3).

John the Baptist was born to prepare the way for his cousin. Jesus came to be the Way – and his coming meant the possibility of a whole new way of being for the people who believed – and who believe – in him.

> O come, O come, Immanuel,
> And ransom captive Israel,
> That mourns in lonely exile here
> Until the Son of God appear.
>
> *Rejoice, rejoice! Immanuel*
> *Shall come to thee, O Israel.*
>
> O come, O come, thou Lord of might
> Who to thy tribes on Sinai's height
> In ancient times didst give the law
> In cloud, and majesty, and awe.
>
> O come, thou Rod of Jesse, free
> Thine own from Satan's tyranny;
> From depths of hell thy people save
> And give them victory o'er the grave.

O come, thou Dayspring, come and cheer
Our spirits by thine advent here;
Disperse the gloomy clouds of night,
And death's dark shadows put to flight.

O come, thou Key of David, come
And open wide our heavenly home;
Make safe the way that leads on high,
And close the path to misery.

(*Christmas Praise* 56)

Personal Reflection

Dear Lord

In you we have a whole new way of being. We no longer belong to this world. We belong to you. Help us to show others what living as a Christian really means. May we show the fruits of the Spirit in our lives and may we never, ever be ashamed of the gospel you have entrusted to us. Amen.

Saturday – 'Incarnation' by John Gowans

The baby cries again this year,
As ev'ry year!
And I must think again of God in Christ.
Again I fear
And comprehend, that's if I can,
How God could wrap himself in man!

If God should want to speak to man,
Say something good,
The words he chose would have to be
Well understood.
One single lovely Word he said
And laid it in a manger bed.

If I have grasped the truth at all,
I've understood
That God once dressed himself in man,
In flesh and blood,
And crossed the gulf of time and space
And came to join the human race!

My finite mind and fumbling thoughts
Still find it hard
To grasp the message printed on
My Christmas card:
That God's sublime salvation plan
In Beth'lem's borrowed barn began!

I can't explain the ageless truth
Of love expressed;
I only know – in Jesus all
The world is blessed.
And when I look into his face
I'm glad God joined the human race!

Something To Do

Make a Christmas card and send it to a friend you haven't talked to for a while.

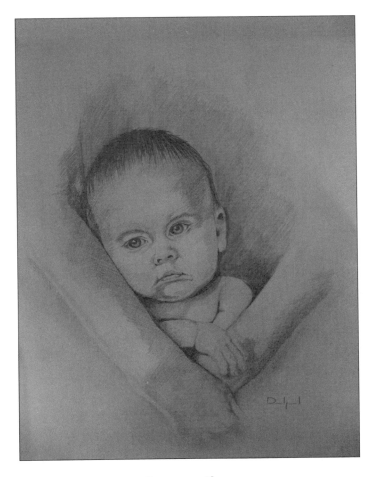

Incarnation

'How God could wrap himself in man'

2nd Sunday – Jesus, Son Of Joseph

If the Church over-exalts Mary, it underestimates Joseph. A study of the family tree of Jesus immediately shows that Joseph was called upon to fulfil a role every bit as unique as Mary's.

In Matthew 1:2-15 the line of David is described in terms of 'the father of …' until verse 16, where Joseph is 'the husband of Mary, of whom [single feminine pronoun in Greek] was born Jesus'.

This deliberate description confirms the doctrine of the virgin birth. Joseph was called upon to raise a child that was not his own. Jesus was on the receiving end of that care. As a consequence he understood the tensions and concerns of step-parents and stepchildren.

In Luke 3:23 the relationship is phrased ambiguously: 'He was the son, so it was thought, of Joseph.' Perhaps Luke perceived the 'nod and wink' of village people who always had doubts as to who Jesus' real father was.

Joseph, coping with the adjustment to first-time parenthood, had no opportunity to settle down and get to know his new wife. Mary had no chance of discovering herself as a mature woman before motherhood was thrust upon her. The boy Jesus may have been subjected to cruel taunts about the identity of his real father.

Yet there was no doubt in the mind of Mary as to the quality of relationship between the three of them.

When she eventually tracked the 12-year-old down in the Temple, she exclaimed: 'Son, why have you treated us like this? Your father and I have been anxiously searching for you' (Luke 2:48). The question is as illuminating as the well-known answer. Not for the first time do we see that Joseph loved Jesus as though he were his own flesh and blood: no man can be anxious *and* apathetic!

Once he had been reassured by the angel (Matthew 1:20-24) Joseph was fully committed to his responsibility as stepfather. He did not desert Mary when he discovered she was pregnant; in all likelihood he was present at the birth. He took charge of the post-birth formalities (Luke 2:21-39), probably paying for the redemption sacrifice (verse 24) himself.

Some time later, probably when Jesus was about 18 months old, Joseph faithfully attended the Passover celebrations (Luke 2:41), and on at least one occasion ensured that Jesus accompanied him (verse 42). Notice that it was not enough to send, Joseph had to attend!

There is another important area in which Joseph gave himself to Jesus: he taught him his trade. In Matthew 13:55 the question is asked: 'Isn't this the carpenter's son?', while Mark's account of the incident reads: 'Isn't this the carpenter?' (Mark 6:3).

We can only ponder the devoted investment of time, love and energy that Jesus received from Joseph. The hours the two spent together. The thrill Joseph must have felt when his pupil had learnt a new skill. The pride he must have taken in his son. The joy at supper time when Jesus recounted to his mother what the men of the house had been doing that day.

In teaching Jesus his craft, Joseph was doing more than sharing a hobby with a son. He was preparing his child in the best way he knew for adult life. More than this, he was preparing Jesus for the day when he, being the first-born, would be the family breadwinner and the head of the family.

Scripture does not reveal when other family members were born, but there were at least six other children (Mark 6:3). They and Mary would need to be provided for. Jesus knew what it was like to struggle for survival.

We do not read of Joseph's death. He was alive when Jesus was 12 years old (Luke 2:42), but is not directly mentioned in the Gospels once the 30-year-old Jesus commenced his ministry (Luke 3:23). The inference of this silence is that Joseph had already died.

If this was indeed the case, Joseph died when Jesus was only a young man. That caring, protecting, practical father gone, just as they were getting to know each other! Jesus experienced the heartbreak of grief. He knew the struggle and heartache of the single-parent family. Despite the chaotic start, Joseph did all he could to provide Jesus with a stable family life. And if Jesus needed that love and influence in his childhood, how much more do our children need security in relationships! They need parents who are prepared to take responsibility for their spiritual development; to take them to worship, not just to send them; to read and pray with them, not just for them.

Surely we dare not invest any less than a wholehearted effort in preparing our children for the harsh realities of adult life. Too easily we can follow the trend to let it be someone else's job – the school's, the Church's, the Army's, the media's.

Do we show enough wisdom and exercise sufficient authority to protect children from the evil slaughter of their innocence?

In considering the humanity of Jesus, we are often led to appreciate his empathy for our general human feelings and failings. But as we look at Jesus as a member of a family, we discover that he experienced some of the deepest emotions of personal relationships, witnessed the tensions of family survival and was, like so many children, a victim of circumstances.

At a time of year when family life features prominently, may we draw strength from the fact that, whatever our domestic circumstances are, Jesus, the son of Joseph, understands.

Nigel Bovey

Monday – Adam

Bible readings: Genesis 1:27; Genesis 2:15-24

'So God created man in his own image, in the image of God he created him; male and female he created them' (Genesis 1:27).

Adam and Eve begin the lineage that leads to Joseph. They begin the story in which we all have a part to play. And, thanks to Jesus, it has a happy ending.

> All hail the power of Jesus' name!
> Let angels prostrate fall;
> Bring forth the royal diadem
> And crown him Lord of all!
>
> Let every kindred, every tribe,
> All nations great and small,
> To him all majesty ascribe,
> And crown him Lord of all!
>
> Ye sinners lost of Adam's race,
> Partakers of the fall,
> Come and be saved by Jesus' grace,
> And crown him Lord of all!
>
> Crown him, ye martyrs of our God
> Who from his altar call;
> Extol the power of Jesus' blood,
> And crown him Lord of all!

O that with yonder sacred throng
We at his feet may fall,
Join in the everlasting song,
And crown him Lord of all!

(SASB 56)

Personal Reflection

Dear heavenly Father

We may begin as sinners lost of Adam's race – but now we are sinners saved by grace – the grace, love and sacrifice of our Lord Jesus Christ. We are still sons of Adam and daughters of Eve but, as they were your children, made in your image, so are we. You are our heavenly Father. Thank you. Amen.

Tuesday – Abraham

Bible readings: Genesis 17:1-8; Genesis 25:7-11

'As for me, this is my covenant with you: You will be the father of many nations. No longer will you be called Abram; your name will be Abraham, for I have made you a father of many nations' (Genesis 17:4-5).

Abraham was a man who had a special everlasting covenant with God. His obedience brought into being the Jewish people. He was indeed a father of many nations and kings did come from his line. In fact the King of kings came from his line.

> The God of Abraham praise,
> Who reigns enthroned above,
> Ancient of everlasting days
> And God of love.
> Jehovah, great I AM,
> By earth and Heaven confessed,
> I bow and bless the sacred name
> Forever blest.
>
> The God of Abraham praise,
> At whose supreme command
> From earth I rise, and seek the joys
> At his right hand.
> I all on earth forsake,
> Its wisdom, fame and power;
> And him my only portion make,
> My shield and tower.
>
> Before the Saviour's face
> The ransomed nations bow,
> O'erwhelmed at his almighty grace

For ever new;
He shows his prints of love,
They kindle to a flame
And sound through all the worlds above:
Worthy the Lamb.

He by himself hath sworn;
I on his oath depend;
I shall, on eagle's wings upborne,
To Heaven ascend.
I shall behold his face,
I shall his powers adore,
And sing the wonders of his grace
For evermore.

The whole triumphant host
Give thanks to God on high;
Hail Father, Son and Holy Ghost,
They ever cry.
Hail Abraham's God and mine!
I join the heavenly lays;
All might and majesty are thine,
And endless praise.

(*SASB* 223)

Personal Reflection

Dear heavenly Father

You were Abraham's God. You are our God. He was obedient. May we be obedient. He was greatly blessed. May we be open to receive all the blessings you want to pour into our lives. Amen.

Wednesday – Ruth

Bible readings: Ruth 1:1-18; Ruth 4:13-17

'Don't urge me to leave you or to turn back from you. Where you go I will go, and where you stay I will stay. Your people will be my people and your God my God. Where you die I will die, and there I will be buried. May the Lord deal with me, be it ever so severely, if anything but death separates you and me' (Ruth 1:16-17).

Ruth played a very important part in Jesus' human genealogy – even though she was a foreigner and a woman! Jews of that time did not count either for very much, if truth be told. But Ruth was willing to leave her own country to accompany Naomi and, eventually, married into the line which would produce not only King David but also King Jesus!

If human hearts are often tender,
And human minds can pity know,
If human love is touched with splendour,
And human hands compassion show,

Then how much more shall God our Father
In love forgive, in love forgive!
Then how much more shall God our Father
Our wants supply, and none deny!

If sometimes men can live for others,
And sometimes give where gifts are spurned,
If sometimes treat their foes as brothers,
And love where love is not returned,

If men will often share their gladness,
If men respond when children cry,
If men can feel each other's sadness,
Each other's tears attempt to dry,

(SASB 50)

Personal Reflection

Dear Lord

What an amazing example of love Ruth gives us! Love that
is willing to sacrifice without any expectation of reward.
Help us to love like that. And we thank you, Lord, that your
love for us led you to make the ultimate sacrifice. Help us
to be worthy of that love. Amen.

Thursday – David

Bible readings: 1 Samuel 16:7; Acts 13:20-22; 1 Samuel 16:13; 1 Samuel 17:45; Psalm 23

'The Lord does not look at the things man looks at. Man looks at the outward appearance, but the Lord looks at the heart' (1 Samuel 16:7).

Shepherd, poet, outlaw, king – and a man after God's own heart. David had his failings as a human being but he was the greatest king Israel ever knew. It was because Joseph was of the house and lineage of David that he had to go to Bethlehem for the census.

> Once, in royal David's city,
> Stood a lowly cattle shed,
> Where a mother laid her baby
> In a manger for his bed.
> Mary was that mother mild,
> Jesus Christ her little child.
>
> He came down to earth from Heaven
> Who is God and Lord of all,
> And his shelter was a stable
> And his cradle was a stall;
> With the poor and mean and lowly
> Lived on earth our Saviour holy.
>
> And through all his wondrous childhood
> He would honour and obey,
> Love and watch the lowly mother
> In whose gentle arms he lay.
> Christian children all must be
> Mild, obedient, good as he.

For he is our childhood's pattern;
Day by day like us he grew;
He was little, weak and helpless;
Tears and smiles like us he knew;
And he feeleth for our sadness,
And he shareth in our gladness.

And our eyes at last shall see him,
Through his own redeeming love;
For that child so dear and gentle
Is our Lord in Heaven above.
And he leads his children on
To the place where he is gone.

(*SASB* 87)

Personal Reflection

Dear Lord

We thank you for the example we have in David of a man with a poet's heart who sought to do your will. He made mistakes – but he found that God was ready and willing to forgive. We thank you, Lord, that if we come to you in true repentance you will forgive. Amen.

Friday – Josiah

Bible reading: 2 Kings 22:1-13

'Josiah was eight years old when he became king, and he reigned in Jerusalem for thirty-one years. His mother's name was Jedidah daughter of Adaiah; she was from Bozkath. He did what was right in the eyes of the Lord and walked in all the ways of his father David, not turning aside to the right or to the left' (2 Kings 22:1-2).

After two very bad kings, Josiah did what was right in God's eyes. During his reign the Book of the Law was rediscovered – after being missing for about 70 years. Josiah repented because the words of the book had been ignored. Then all his people repented and the nation turned back to God. It didn't last beyond Josiah's reign – but he was another good king in Jesus' line.

Don't assume that God's dismissed you from his mind,
Don't assume that God's forgotten to be kind;
For no matter what you do, his love still follows you;
Don't think that you have left him far behind.

For his love remains the same,
He knows you by your name,
Don't think because you failed him he despairs;
For he gives to those who ask
His grace for every task,
God plans for you in love for he still cares.

Don't assume that God will plan for you no more,
Don't assume that there's no future to explore;
For your life he'll re-design, the pattern be divine;
Don't think that your repentance he'll ignore.

Don't assume you cannot give what he'll demand,
Don't assume that God condemns you out of hand;
For he gives to those who ask his grace for every task;
Don't think that God will fail to understand.

(*SASB* 44)

Personal Reflection

Dear heavenly Father

We thank you for the example we have in Josiah of someone who followed you with all his heart and did what was right in your eyes. And his influence inspired his whole nation to repent and turn to you. We might not have that much influence but we all have some. Help us to lead the people close to us to focus on you. Amen.

Saturday – 'Homeless' by John Gowans

He has no home except this grimy street
Which wears the winter like a shapeless shroud.
He has no friend, except the witless one
Who walks beside him through the thoughtless crowd.

He has no food but what his fingers find
Among the garbage which the dogs disdain.
He has no hope to help him through the day,
No one to ease his lonely night of pain.

Does no one care? Is no one moved enough
To throw a blanket round his bony form?
Will no one put some bread into his hand,
Protect his head against the stinging storm?

I care! … says Christ. I know what 'homeless' means.
I'm with the hungry in the line for beans!
I know the pitted pavement of the street,
And Skid Row bears the imprint of my feet.
I've often had no place to lay my head;
At Bethlehem they borrowed me a bed!

You want to find me? Then you'd better come
And face the stinking of the city slum,
Where men live daily wishing they were dead,
And give away their dignity for bread.

You have the gall to ask me if I care?
Come down to Desp'rate Street, you'll find me there!
And grasp this truth, for it could set you free:
All that you do for them, you do for me.

Something To Do

Pray specifically for homeless people who will have no home in which to celebrate Christmas.

Homeless

'He has no home except this grimy street'

3rd Sunday – Jesus, Son Of Man

There is a haunting beauty in the title which Jesus chose to use for himself – Son of man. Others called him Lord or Teacher and, in later writings, he was to be known as Prince of Glory, Lord of lords and King of kings. But when Jesus referred to himself, it was with the unpretentious title Son of man.

Whatever associations the name might have had for some with ancient prophetic writings, for most of his contemporaries and for ourselves the title speaks of his essential humanity. Divine, yes, but also truly and properly human. A son of man who had nowhere to lay his head (Luke 9:58). A son of man who had come to seek and to save (Luke 19:10). A son of man who knew hunger and thirst and tiredness.

And it is on his full-blooded humanity that we focus in this Advent meditation as we prepare our hearts and minds to celebrate his coming. The title has significance for each of us.

The title Son of man tells me that Jesus is my brother. God could have revealed himself in thunder and lightning or by some awesome miraculous break in the natural order of things. He could have appeared magnificently on earth as, according to fable, the gods of mythology did from time to time. He could have matched the wildest imaginings of Messianic hopes.

But instead he came as a son of man. Born to a humble family in a humble place. A son of man who for the first 30 years of his life might well have been indistinguishable from any other godly youth of his time – a true son of man.

When I open my heart to receive again the Christ of Christmas he will not come as the Lord of lords or King of kings, but in the simplicity of a son of man. When I sit down to share with him, I will not be facing someone from another universe. I will be talking to my brother. Someone who was not only tempted in all ways like ourselves, but someone who knows and understands the demands, pressures and conflicts of life from first-hand experience.

Jesus has seen human life from the inside. There is nothing new about human life that I can tell him. He has been through it all himself. That in itself is a strengthening thought.

The title Son of man reminds me that Jesus is my ideal, my supreme example. 'In him I see the man I want to be,' sings Peter in the musical *Son of Man*. In him we see humanity as it is supposed to be and the human life lived as it was meant to be lived.

The Early Church frequently spoke of him as the Second Adam – and the thought-picture is clear. In Jesus, humanity was restored to what it once had been. And because we are human we can identify with that picture. In Jesus we see the ideal for our own lives.

The trouble with films like *The Last Temptation Of Christ* is that they take a perfectly good truth too far – the classic definition of a heresy. That film stresses the humanity of Jesus, but loses all sense of balance. The humanity depicted is not that of Jesus of the Gospels, but the humanity of someone like ourselves.

The mind recoils from the suggestion that, at the end of viewing the film, the audience might be invited to sing the chorus 'To be like Jesus, this hope possesses me'. Would anyone want to be like that Jesus?

The humanity we see in the true Jesus is not a reflection of ourselves with all our weaknesses, but rather humanity lifted to its highest degree. It is the humanity which Paul captures in his portrait of love in 1 Corinthians 13 – surely a portrait of Jesus himself:

'Love is patient; love is kind and envies no one. Love is never boastful, nor conceited, nor rude; never selfish, not quick to take offence. Love keeps no score of wrongs; does not gloat over other men's sins, but delights in the truth. There is nothing love cannot face; there is no limit to its faith, its hope, and its endurance' (verses 4-7 *NEB*).

That kind of humanity is not an abstract ideal. Because I see it embodied in Jesus, my brother, the Son of man, I find myself drawn towards that ideal. The hope kindles within that I might be like him.

The title Son of man speaks to me not only of a brother and an ideal of humanity, but also of someone who will help me attain. He became one of us in order to help us become like him.

Seen from his human side there is no great unbridgeable chasm between Jesus and ourselves. He is one of us – with a difference. And the difference is that we are only partially and incompletely filled with God the Holy Spirit – the Spirit whom the Early Church soon began to call the Spirit of Jesus because he reminded them of everything Jesus had stood for. Jesus was perfectly and completely filled with the Spirit. 'In him dwelleth all the fulness of the Godhead bodily,' as Paul put it (Colossians 2:9 *KJV*).

That Jesus was the Man, the Son of man, perfectly filled with the Spirit – a picture I have developed elsewhere – whereas we are still imperfectly filled, is a truth that should fill us with joy and with holy ambition. It is possible to be like him. He is not wholly other. We share humanity together – and we share together an experience, however humbly, of the Spirit. With 'his Spirit helping me, like him I'll be'.

There is a shortage of Christmas carols that speak of the Son of man. But once the full significance of the title grips us, a new spontaneous carol of praise will sound from the heart.

John Larsson

Monday – Here is my servant

Bible readings: Isaiah 42:1-9; Philippians 2:5-7

'Your attitude should be the same as that of Christ Jesus: Who, being in very nature God, did not consider equality with God something to be grasped, but made himself nothing, taking the very nature of a servant, being made in human likeness' (Philippians 2:5-7).

Jesus did not come as a conquering king – although he could have done so. He came as a servant – ready and willing to do what his Father wanted him to do.

> Master, speak: thy servant heareth,
> Waiting for thy gracious word,
> Longing for thy voice that cheereth;
> Master, let it now be heard.
> I am listening, Lord, for thee;
> What hast thou to say to me?
>
> Speak to me by name, O Master,
> Let me know it is to me.
> Speak, that I may follow faster,
> With a step more firm and free,
> Where the shepherd leads the flock
> In the shadow of the rock.
>
> Master, speak: though least and lowest,
> Let me not unheard depart.
> Master, speak! for O thou knowest
> All the yearning of my heart,
> Knowest all its truest need;
> Speak! and make me blest indeed.

Master, speak: and make me ready,
When thy voice is truly heard,
With obedience glad and steady
Still to follow every word.
I am listening, Lord, for thee;
Master, speak: O speak to me!

(*SASB* 614)

Personal Reflection

Dear Lord

Help us to serve others. Sometimes we are too full of our own importance to look at the needs of the people around us. Please, help us to put others first and to give them the best that is in us. Amen.

Tuesday – I am the Lord's servant

Bible readings: Luke 1:26-38; Luke 1:46-49

'And Mary said: "My soul glorifies the Lord and my spirit rejoices in God my Saviour, for he has been mindful of the humble state of his servant. From now on all generations will call me blessed, for the Mighty One has done great things for me – holy is his name"' (Luke 1:46-49).

In spite of all the implications, Mary said yes to what God wanted of her. She considered herself to be the Lord's servant and, as such, would obey him implicitly. Can the same be said of our obedience when the Lord wants us to do something difficult and/or life-changing?

I bring thee, dear Jesus, my all,
Nor hold back from thee any part;
Obedient to thy welcome call,
I yield thee the whole of my heart.

O speak, O speak while before thee I pray!
And, O Lord, just what seemeth thee good
Reveal, and my heart shall obey.

Perverse, stubborn once was my will.
My feet ran in self-chosen ways;
Thy pleasure henceforth to fulfil,
I'll spend all the rest of my days.

The doubts that have darkened my soul,
The shame and the fears that I hate,
O banish, and bid me be whole,
A clean heart within me create!

O give me a heart that is true,
Unspotted and pure in thy sight,
A love that would anything do,
A life given up to the fight!

(*SASB* 422)

Personal Reflection

Dear Lord

Help us to be obedient. You might want us to go to places we have never been to do things we have never done and that might well make us uncomfortable. But we can trust you implicitly, Lord. Help us to remember that. Amen.

Wednesday – The servant of all

Bible readings: Mark 9:33-37; Mark 10:43-45; John 13:12-17; 2 Corinthians 4:5-6

'Whoever wants to be great among you must be your servant, and whoever wants to be first must be slave of all. For even the Son of Man did not come to be served, but to serve, and to give his life as a ransom for many' (Mark 10:43-45).

As Christians, our task in the world is to be servants. Jesus gave us the example. We have to follow that example if we want to follow Jesus.

> Kneeling before thee, Lord, I am praying,
> Claiming a closer communion with thee,
> Longing to sever from selfish ambition;
> Break thou each fetter and set my soul free.
>
> *Into thy hands, Lord, take me and mould me,*
> *E'en as the potter handles the clay;*
> *Make me a vessel fit for thy service;*
> *Cleanse me and fill me, and use me today.*
>
> Fruitless has been the way of my choosing;
> Now I am leaving the future with thee;
> Treading the pathway of joyful obedience,
> Lord, see me ready thy servant to be.

Not in my own strength can I accomplish
All thou art planning for me, day by day;
Owning the limit of human endeavour,
Humbly I seek, Lord, the grace to obey.

(SASB 501)

Personal Reflection

Dear Lord

Are we fit for your service or is there still work to be done within us? Help us to be willing to be moulded by you so that we can be the kind of servants you want us to be. Amen.

Thursday – Live as servants of God

Bible readings: John 12:23-26; Matthew 25:14-30

'Whoever serves me must follow me; and where I am, my servant also will be. My Father will honour the one who serves me' (John 12:26).

Whatever God entrusts to us in this world we must work so that we will hear him say to us, 'Well done, good and faithful servant!'

> On God's word relying,
> Every doubt defying,
> Faith is heard replying;
> Praise God, I believe!
>
> *I believe in God the Father,*
> *I believe in God the Son;*
> *I believe in the Holy Spirit,*
> *Blessèd Godhead, Three in One;*
> *I believe in a full salvation,*
> *In redemption through the blood;*
> *I believe I'll receive a crown of life,*
> *When I hear the Lord's: Well done.*
>
> Confidence unshaken;
> When bereft, forsaken,
> E'en if life be taken,
> Praise God, I believe!

Peace and joy unending
In my soul are blending,
Faith on love depending,
Praise God, I believe!

(*SASB* 222)

Personal Reflection

Dear Lord

We want to hear you say 'well done' to us. What we have to do may not be easy but we pray that you will keep us faithful and willing to do your work. Amen.

Friday – I have called you friends

Bible reading: John 15:1-17

'I no longer call you servants, because a servant does not know his master's business. Instead, I have called you friends, for everything that I learned from my Father I have made known to you. You did not choose me, but I chose you and appointed you to go and bear fruit – fruit that will last. Then the Father will give you whatever you ask in my name. This is my command: Love each other' (John 15:15-17).

What an incredible privilege to be called Jesus' friends! But we have to remember that with privilege comes responsibility.

Many are the things I cannot understand,
All above me mystery I see;
But the gift most wonderful from God's own hand
Surely is his gift of grace to me!

Higher than the stars that reach eternity,
Broader than the boundaries of endless space,
Is the boundless love of God that pardoned me;
O the wonder of his grace!

When I came to Jesus with my sin and shame
And to him confessed my deepest need,
When by faith I trusted fully in his name,
God's rich grace was granted me indeed.

Passing understanding is his boundless love,
More than I can ever comprehend,
Jesus, in his mercy, left his throne above,
All to be my Saviour and my friend.

(SASB 52)

Personal Reflection

Dear Father God

We can't really understand your love but we can be grateful for it. And how grateful we are, too, that Jesus came to this earth to be our Saviour and friend! Help us to love each other and reach out to others with that love. Amen.

Saturday – 'Co-worker' by John Gowans

Your work within your world
Is something stunning.
I do not see the half
But I'm impressed.
I glimpse the edges
Of your vast designings,
I feel the rim
And wonder at the rest!

You call me 'fellow-worker'!
Lord, that's funny!
The title strikes a humoristic note,
When often all I do
Is pass your spanner,
And now and then
You let me hold your coat!

Co-worker

'And now and then you let me hold your coat!'

161

Something To Do

See if there is some practical work you can do in the coming week. Is there a house-bound person for whom you could do some shopping? A neighbour for whom you could babysit for an evening?

4th Sunday – Jesus, Son Of God

All the biblical titles ascribed to Jesus are precious to those who love him and they all contribute to our understanding of the wonder and mystery of his being. So it has been good to see him in his historical perspective as son of David, in the family setting at Nazareth as son of Joseph, and, in the words Jesus loved to use of himself, Son of man.

But, important and illuminating as all these descriptions are, they do not bear unmistakable testimony to that divine dimension so essential to our worship, faith and hope; to that truth we rejoice in singing about in the words of the carol:

> *Veiled in flesh the Godhead see:*
> *Hail the incarnate Deity!*

For this vital dimension we rely very much indeed on the title 'Son of God'.

Why was it so important for the Church in the first few centuries of the Christian era to spell out the humanity and deity of Jesus Christ, expressed for Salvationists in their fourth doctrine: 'We believe that in the person of Jesus Christ the Divine and human natures are united, so that he is truly and properly God and truly and properly man'?

In brief, it was because this belief witnesses to two fundamental truths. Firstly, that in human flesh Jesus revealed all we can conceive of the character of God. Secondly, that in Jesus God was at work for our salvation, as so beautifully expressed by Paul: 'God was in Christ, reconciling the world unto himself' (2 Corinthians 5:19, all references in this article from *King James Version*).

163

The roots of the title Son of God can be seen in the pages of the Old Testament. In Hosea 11:1 we see the nation of Israel being called God's son: 'When Israel was a child, then I loved him, and called my son out of Egypt.' The kings of Israel, especially those who were descendants of David, also bore this title.

But in the New Testament, with reference to Jesus, the title carried a much more profound meaning, indicating nothing less than the intimate oneness that existed between Jesus and the Father. So Luke 2:49 records the words of the boy Jesus in the Temple: 'Wist ye not that I must be about my Father's business?'

The parable in Mark 12:1-11 shows us Jesus speaking of the 'one son, his wellbeloved' (verse 6). And consider the statement recorded slightly differently by both Matthew and Luke (10:22): 'All things are delivered unto me of my Father: and no man knoweth the Son, but the Father; neither knoweth any man the Father, save the Son, and he to whomsoever the Son will reveal him' (Matthew 11:27).

This revelation of what is meant by the title Son of God is further developed in John's Gospel, considered by most scholars to have been written some time after the first three 'synoptic' Gospels and to have been the fruit of long meditation and thought. In John Chapter 1 we have the great presentation of the coming in full humanity of the eternal Word: 'And the Word was made flesh' (verse 14). Later, there are explicit statements, such as 'I and my Father are one' (10:30) and 'He that hateth me hateth my Father also' (15:23).

The theme continues elsewhere, for example in Hebrews 1:1, 2: 'God ... Hath in these last days spoken unto us by his Son, whom he hath appointed heir of all things, by whom also he made the worlds.'

So the Bible proclaims that Jesus was not just a great teacher, not even the greatest of teachers. Neither was he simply the noblest man who ever walked on this earth. He was the Son of God. He was one with God himself.

And as such he was able to reveal to us what God is like. John records Jesus saying to Philip at the Last Supper: 'Have I been so long time with you, and yet hast thou not known me, Philip? he that hath seen me hath seen the Father' (John 14:9).

What a comfort and a challenge this is! The comfort lies in the revelation of God as a loving Father, and the challenge in his requirement that we should be like Jesus and follow in his footsteps.

If this would overwhelm us we may rejoice further that this Son of God came to be our saviour, and 'being found in fashion as a man, he humbled himself, and became obedient unto death, even the death of the cross' (Philippians 2:8).

Man of sorrows! what a name
For the Son of God, who came
Ruined sinners to reclaim;
Hallelujah! what a Saviour!

Lyndon Taylor

Monday – Celebrate because Jesus was born on earth

Bible reading: Luke 2:1-20

'While they were there, the time came for the baby to be born, and she gave birth to her firstborn, a son. She wrapped him in cloths and placed him in a manger, because there was no room for them in the inn' (Luke 2:6-7).

It is an amazing thought – Jesus made the incredibly long journey from the glories of Heaven to a humble stable. And he made that journey because of love – the love he has for each one of us. What a reason to celebrate!

Thou didst leave thy throne and thy kingly crown
When thou camest to earth for me;
But in Bethlehem's home was there found no room
For thy holy nativity.

O come to my heart, Lord Jesus;
There is room in my heart for thee.

Heaven's arches rang when the angels sang,
Proclaiming thy royal degree;
But of lowly birth cam'st thou, Lord, on earth
And in great humility.

Thou camest, O Lord, with the living word
That should set thy people free;
But with mocking scorn, and with crown of thorn,
They bore thee to Calvary.

When Heaven's arches ring, and her choirs shall sing,
At thy coming to victory,
Let thy voice call me home, saying: Yet there is room,
There is room at my side for thee!

And my heart shall rejoice, Lord Jesus,
When thou comest and callest for me.

(*SASB* 101)

Personal Reflection

Dear Lord

Just at this moment we celebrate the fact that you were willing to leave Heaven to come to earth. If you hadn't done that there would be no hope for us at all. So, thank you, Jesus. And thank you, too, that you have promised us that one day we will be in your presence. Amen.

Tuesday – Celebrate because he loved us enough to die for us

Bible readings: John 17:1-5; 13-19; 19:28-30

'Father, the time has come. Glorify your Son, that your Son may glorify you' (John 17:1).

Jesus came to this earth to reconcile people to God. The only way to do that was to die for us. Because he was willing to do that, we now have the right to be called children of God.

Who is he in yonder stall,
At whose feet the shepherds fall?

'Tis the Lord! O wondrous story,
'Tis the Lord, the King of Glory!
At his feet we humbly fall,
Crown him, crown him Lord of all!

Who is he in deep distress,
Fasting in the wilderness?

Who is he to whom they bring
All the sick and sorrowing?

Who is he on yonder tree
Dies in grief and agony?

Who is he who from the grave
Comes to succour, help and save?

Who is he who from his throne
Rules through all the worlds alone?

(*SASB* 104)

Personal Reflection

Dear Jesus

As we think about the whole story of what you did for us we can hardly take it in. Today we celebrate the fact that you loved us enough to die for us – to sacrifice yourself so that we could be forgiven and saved. Thank you. Amen.

Wednesday – Celebrate because he sent us the Holy Spirit

Bible readings: John 15:15-21; Acts 1:1-8; 2:1-4; Romans 15:13

'May the God of hope fill you with all joy and peace as you trust in him, so that you may overflow with hope by the power of the Holy Spirit' (Romans 15:13).

The Holy Spirit lives within us so that we have a constant link with God. The Holy Spirit gives us strength, guidance, help, comfort, power – and so much more besides. Another great reason to celebrate!

> Who is it tells me what to do
> And helps me to obey?
> Who is it plans the route for me
> And will not let me stray?
> Who is it tells me when to speak
> And what I ought to say?
>
> *That's the Spirit! Holy Spirit!*
> *That's the Spirit of the Lord in me!*
>
> Who is it gives me heavy loads
> And helps me take the strain?
> Who is it calls to sacrifice
> And helps me bear the pain?
> Who is it sees me when I fall
> And lifts me up again?

Who is it shows me what to be
And leads me to that goal?
Who is it claims the heart of me
And wants to take control?
Who is it calls to holiness
Of body, mind and soul?

(*SASB* 204)

Personal Reflection

Dear Jesus

When you left earth you promised that the Holy Spirit would come – and he did with wind and flame. Thank you for the helper, guide and comforter who dwells within God's children. Today we celebrate that he is a living presence in the world. Amen.

Thursday – Celebrate because we have a guidebook

Bible readings: Psalm 119:97-105; Proverbs 30:5; Isaiah 40:8; Ephesians 6:17; Hebrews 4:12-13

'Your word is a lamp to my feet and a light for my path' (Psalm 119:105).

We have the Bible to help and guide us along our life path. It is full of words of wisdom and messages of hope and love. If we make it a part of our lives we will be immeasurably enriched.

> Break thou the bread of life,
> O Lord, to me,
> As thou didst break the loaves
> Beside the sea;
> Beyond the sacred page
> I seek thee, Lord;
> My spirit pants for thee,
> O living Word!
>
> Thou art the bread of life,
> O Lord, to me,
> Thy holy word the truth
> That saveth me;
> Give me to eat and live
> With thee above;
> Teach me to love thy truth,
> For thou art love.

O send thy Spirit, Lord,
Now unto me,
That he may touch my eyes
And make me see;
Show me the truth concealed
Within thy word,
And in thy book revealed
I see the Lord.

(*SASB* 650)

Personal Reflection

Dear Father God

We thank you that we have the Bible to help us and guide us on our Christian path. Today we celebrate your word that can speak to us and our situation just as cogently now as it has for thousands of years. Thank you. Amen.

Friday – Celebrate because we are invited to a great party!

Bible readings: Matthew 8:11; Luke 14:15-24; Revelation 3:20; 19:6-9

'Blessed are those who are invited to the wedding supper of the Lamb!' (Revelation 19:9).

We are invited to the greatest party of all time – the wedding supper of the Lamb! But we don't have to wait until then to share in fellowship with Jesus and to celebrate knowing him and loving him – and knowing that he loves us. That can happen at any time.

My God, I am thine;
What a comfort divine,
What a blessing to know that my Jesus is mine!

Hallelujah, send the glory!
Hallelujah, amen!
Hallelujah, send the glory!
Revive us again.

In the heavenly Lamb
Thrice happy I am,
And my heart it doth dance at the sound of his name.

True pleasures abound
In the rapturous sound,
And whoever has found it hath Paradise found.

My Jesus to know,
And feel his blood flow,
'Tis life everlasting, 'tis Heaven below.

Yet onward I haste
To the heavenly feast,
That, that is the fulness, but this is the taste.

And this I shall prove,
Till with joy I remove
To the Heaven of heavens in Jesus' love.

(*SASB* 355)

Personal Reflection

Dear Lord

Today we celebrate the thought of the greatest party ever –
the wedding supper of the Lamb! And we all have
invitations. Hallelujah! Amen.

Saturday – 'Mercy Seat?' by John Gowans

Is this the mercy seat,
This manger place
Which seems so full of love,
Of good, of grace?

And will God talk to me,
Tell me his will,
Here, wrapped in silences,
So soft, so still?

I touch this tiny hand,
I see this face;
The God I'm looking for
Is in this place.

My heart prepares itself
Its Lord to greet,
And kneels with joy before
This mercy seat.

And must I bring a gift,
Some worth, some wealth?
Is it enough for me
To give myself?

Give him your yesterdays,
Tomorrows too.
He asks for nothing else
But you!
Just you!

Something To Do

Find a quiet space this weekend where you can just sit and listen to God speaking to you.

Mercy Seat?

'My heart prepares itself its Lord to meet'

Epiphany

The feast of Epiphany, which is observed on 6 January, is an older celebration than Christmas and marks the visit of the Magi to Bethlehem. Epiphany means 'manifestation'.

'Lucky for some!' said the young Salvationist in the Bible study group. He was talking about the wise men. 'They had a star to guide them. If only it was that easy for me!'

You have to sympathise. It's hard not to envy those sages from the east. After all, haven't we all, at times, looked in vain for a 'sign in the sky'? Wouldn't you welcome the occasional bright light to dispel the fog of your uncertainty? Or submit to a timely signal that could show you which way to go and arrest you when you are on the wrong track? Or accept a clear vision that would direct you to the right choice and prevent you from plumping for the wrong one?

Who wouldn't like to be guided like that?

But was it really that easy for the wise men? Was God's way of guiding them that different from the way he guides us? Were there no moments of uncertainty and no wrong turnings along the way?

The magi of the Nativity story were probably not the only sincere, God-fearing, wise people who had a feeling that something special was about to happen in the history of humankind. There must have been others.

But for his purpose, God needed just this handful (tradition says three because they had three gifts). The others had to wait until a later day for the good news to reach their shores.

The wise men weren't like the astrologers and confidence tricksters who sold horoscopes in the marketplaces, fatalists who said that your fate is fixed by the positions of the stars. Or like New Agers who believe that the human will matters little because people are under the control of invisible cosmic forces, whether they like it or not.

Rather than the focus of superstitious speculation, to the wise men the stars would have been mainly a source of practical information – their chart, compass and calendar. They consulted the stars when planning to sow a field, embark on a journey or fix an important date.

Looking at the skies was part of their daily routine – and that is where God chose to meet them. He spoke to them not through the unknown, but the known. They were familiar with the stars and the appearance of an extra one aroused their curiosity. God usually comes to us in the familiar things.

He spoke to Zechariah, the father of John the Baptist, during the familiar routine at the Temple. He gave Moses the encouragement he needed by taking the shepherd's staff which Moses had been using for years. David defeated Goliath with the familiar sling, not the unfamiliar sword. Peter the fisherman was taught a much-needed lesson about faith as he sat in his fishing boat holding his own fishing net.

So don't worry if you haven't experienced anything out of the ordinary – this or that blessing or a mighty sign. God will guide you, but he is probably going to do it through ways that are much closer to hand, and especially through the routine of your daily life.

He may also use those very ordinary meetings; or a Bible reading you have read many times before; or those apparently uneventful quiet moments of prayer; or a happy relationship (or an awkward relationship!); or that unspectacular gift or talent you are inclined to take for granted; or that task that nobody else seems willing to tackle. Or in many, many other ways.

And none of them is 'second best' to the star the wise men followed.

The star did not turn them into remote-controlled robots. At times they lost sight of it and had to look elsewhere for help. They even made the mistake – fatal for some – of visiting King Herod.

Doing God's will does not mean that we are on 'automatic pilot'. We still have to think, decide, use our own wills. It means using every resource available – our experience, knowledge, common sense, friendships and earnest prayer. It means we will always – thankfully – remain human and therefore vulnerable to error.

But it also means that with perseverance we will, like the wise men, reach the goal.

Mike Marvell